A Guide to 200 Best-Selling Picture Books

WHAT SHOULD
I READ ALOUD?

Nancy A. Anderson

INTERNATIONAL
Reading Association
®
800 BARKSDALE ROAD, PO BOX 8139
NEWARK, DE 19714-8139, USA
www.reading.org

W9-AOG-865

Executive Editor, Books   Corinne M. Mooney
Developmental Editor   Charlene M. Nichols
Developmental Editor   Tori Mello Bachman
Developmental Editor   Stacey Lynn Sharp
Editorial Production Manager   Shannon T. Fortner
Design and Composition Manager   Anette Schuetz

Project Editors   Charlene M. Nichols and Rebecca A. Fetterolf

Cover   Design and Illustration, Thomson Digital

Library of Congress Cataloging-in-Publication Data

Anderson, Nancy A.
  What should I read aloud? : a guide to 200 best-selling picture books / Nancy A. Anderson.
      p. cm.
  Includes bibliographical references and index.
  ISBN-13: 978-0-87207-679-2
  1. Children--Books and reading--United States. 2. Picture books for children--United States. 3. Children's literature--Study and teaching (Early childhood)--United States. 4. Reading--Parent participation--United States. I. Title.
  Z1037.A1A66 2007
  011.62--dc22

                                                                                                    2007020348

Book cover from *Goodnight Moon* by Margaret Wise Brown, illustrated by Clement Hurd. © 1947 by Harper & Row. Text © renewed 1975 by Roberta Brown Rauch. Illustrations © renewed 1975 by Edith Hurd, Clement Hurd, John Thacher Hurd, and George Hellyer, as Trustees of the Edith & Clement Hurd 1982 Trust. Used by permission of HarperCollins Publishers.

This book is dedicated to Boogie Bear and Rachel Baby,
for your unconditional love.

Contents

About the Author

Nancy A. Anderson is an associate professor in the Department of Childhood Education and Literacy Studies at the University of South Florida, Tampa, Florida, USA. She teaches courses in children's literature, literacy, and technology. She completed her bachelor's degree in Elementary Education at New Mexico State University, Las Cruces, New Mexico, USA, and her master's and doctorate in Curriculum and Instruction, reading emphasis, at the University of Southern Mississippi, Hattiesburg, Mississippi, USA.

She is the author of the textbook *Elementary Children's Literature: The Basics for Teachers and Parents* (2006), which is now in its second edition with Allyn & Bacon. She has contributed book chapters in *Literacy Assessment for Today's Schools* (1995) and *Pathways for Literacy: Learners Teach and Teachers Learn* (1994), both published by the College Reading Association. Additionally, she has published numerous articles on children's literature and reading education in journals such as *Bookbird: A Journal of International Children's Literature, The Dragon Lode, Journal of Reading Education, Reading Horizons, Reading Research and Instruction,* and *The Reading Teacher.*

Author Information for Correspondence and Workshops
If you have questions or comments, please write
to naa11@verizon.net.

Illustration from *The Tale of Peter Rabbit* by Beatrix Potter. © 1902, renewed 2002 by Frederick Warne & Co. Ltd. Reproduced by permission of Frederick Warne & Co. Ltd.

Preface

If you loved to read, or be read to, as a child, you probably would like to share some of your favorite childhood books with your own children. However, you may have forgotten the titles or never paid attention to the authors' names. If so, you may have gone into a library or bookstore and asked something like, "Do you have the book about the machine that was in a race against time and ended up in the cellar of a new building?"

Or perhaps you asked, "Could you help me find the book about the stuffed toy in a department store that lost a button?" If you were lucky, you had a librarian or salesperson who had also read your favorite childhood books and could take you to them, but more than likely, you faced a blank stare. If so, this book is for you. In this book, you will find 200 of the best-selling picture books published from 1902 through 2005. By reading the book descriptions, you can identify your favorite childhood books, and you can also locate newer books that you want to share with children.

I have also written this book for teachers and parents who want to read to young children and encourage them to read on their own but who want guidance on which books to select out of more than 50,000 children's books in print (and more than 5,000 new titles published yearly). As an author of a children's literature textbook (Anderson, 2006a), I often have parents ask me, "What are the best books to read to my children?" "What books should I purchase for them?" and "What books should they be reading?" Newspaper reporters have even asked me, "What is a recommended list of summer reading for children?" My personal list of favorites contains several hundred books, but I want to answer these questions with a reasonable list of suggested reading so I do not overwhelm people with their choices.

To help teachers and parents make good selections, I have analyzed sales trends of children's trade books (books sold to consumers), noting which have sold the most copies over the past 100-plus years. I believe that if a multitude of other teachers, parents, and librarians have purchased certain children's books, those books must be highly appealing to children and adults alike and, therefore, make excellent choices for a beginning list of books to read. Within this book, I describe 200 best-selling picture books, giving emphasis to those I believe are of high literary quality that would appeal to today's children.

The primary source I used in selecting titles for inclusion in this book is the research conducted by *Publishers Weekly*, which periodically compiles self-reported data from children's book publishers (see Roback, 2003; Roback, Britton, & Hochman, 2001). While many books are featured on the multitude of weekly bestsellers lists (see Truitt, 1998), to qualify as an all-time best-selling book, total sales since the original date of publication must exceed 750,000 copies according to *Publishers Weekly*, the primary news source for people in the book industry, such as publishers, booksellers, and librarians.

To keep my list of bestsellers up-to-date with great books published since the last time publishers reported their data, I regularly review the weekly children's bestsellers lists on the websites for *Publishers Weekly* (http://www.publishersweekly.com) and *The New York Times* (http://www.nytimes.com/pages/books/bestseller/index.html). I also periodically review the *USA Today* bestsellers website (http://asp.usatoday.com/life/books/booksdatabase/default.aspx), although their list does not separate the children's from the adult books, making it less useful in the analysis of children's literature.

Authors of other publications that provide a cadre of recommended children's books base their choices either on awards that a small group of adults has selected or on the taste of the individual who compiled the list, determined by her or his own definition of quality literature, which varies widely. What makes this book different from other recommended reading lists is that the featured books do not represent the favorites of a single person, nor do they represent the choices of a small committee that bestows book awards. Rather, the children's books I include have, in effect, been given a people's choice award because they were the books most frequently purchased by people much like you—parents, grandparents, and educators.

People purchase the timeless books they loved as children for their own children. In addition, they purchase more recently published books that teachers, parents, and librarians recommend—not because a distinguished person in the education field says they are good, or because a book award says they are good, but because *children* say they are good.

I have long seen the need for a book that compiles the canon of childhood literary treasures. The Reading First Initiative, a component of the No

Child Left Behind Act of 2001, targets reading achievement for children in high-poverty, low-achieving schools—the population that is least likely to experience these books at home. Educators in early intervention programs may find this book useful in selecting titles to share with youngsters in this population and for recommending selections for parents who typically share only books with familiar television and movie characters.

U.S. administrators have responded to the accountability sanctions of the No Child Left Behind Act by increasingly emphasizing literacy achievement, starting in preschool. However, even preschool (typically children ages 3–4) is not early enough if the goal is for all children to succeed. Children develop much of their capacity for learning in the first three years of life, when their brains grow to 90% of their eventual adult weight (Karoly, Greenwood, Sanders, & Chiesa, 1998). Yet, reading lists for these age groups are rare, despite the belief that the term *emergent reader* is generally used in reference to children from birth to age 9 (Botzakis & Malloy, 2006). To help fill this gap, I have devoted chapter 3 to literature for children from birth through age 2 and chapter 4 to ages 3–4. Subsequent chapters are devoted to books for children ages 5–8.

Descriptions of each of the 200 children's picture books include complete title, names of author and illustrator (when only one name appears, the author is also the illustrator), year of original publication, current publisher, and number of pages. I follow this with a synopsis of the book.

It is difficult for me to pigeonhole books to specific age levels, but because parents and beginning teachers have asked me to do this numerous times, I have organized chapters by *suggested* age levels to give you general guidance. Within each of the age-level chapters, I have further grouped books by topic or theme.

All 200 picture books were still in print while I wrote this book; however, a few may have gone out of print by the time it reaches you. Nonetheless, those books may still be available in libraries, and you may be able to purchase them from bookstores on the Internet that sell used books, such as Amazon.com, ABEBooks.com, Alibris.com, or Bookfinder.com. In addition, you might even find a few of these treasures in the old trunk of childhood items your parents saved for you in the attic.

At the end of this book, you will find a glossary of the literacy terms used in this book. The glossary is followed by two indexes: names and titles, and subjects (topics, themes, and genres). The subject index should be especially useful for educators who teach through thematic instruction and for parents who homeschool their children.

For children to obtain the greatest enjoyment from your reading sessions, I have included information on how best to share books with young children (see chapter 1) and how you can help them learn to read while doing so (see chapter 2). In summary, the following features of this book will help you to make excellent choices when selecting picture books:

- This book is written especially for teachers and parents who want guidance on which picture books to select.
- It contains descriptions of best-selling picture books—both old and new.
- Titles were selected for inclusion based on the volume of sales, rather than the tastes of a single individual or small committee.
- Books are grouped by suggested age levels.
- Books are annotated with title, author, illustrator, original copyright year, current publisher, and page length, followed by a synopsis.
- Information is included on how best to share picture books with young children as well as how to help them learn to read the books on their own.
- An end-of-book glossary provides a quick reference for unfamiliar literacy terms.
- Comprehensive indexes feature titles, authors, illustrators, and subjects.

For those who are thinking about what children should read after picture books, I have planned two more books. The next books in this series will target readers ages 8–12 and readers ages 13–18.

I hope this book will open avenues for you and the children in your life to spend many enjoyable hours together with books and that their reading ability and understanding of life will increase because of this.

Acknowledgments

I give sincere thanks to both my internal and external reviewers for their outstanding feedback and many fine suggestions for improvement: Elizabeth

Larkin, University of South Florida, Sarasota, Florida, USA; Carolyn Eichenberger, Godard School at Pickerington, Ohio, USA; Wendy Kasten, Kent State University, Kent, Ohio, USA; Jan Lewis, Pacific Lutheran University, Tacoma, Washington, USA; and Karen A. Brucken, Parma City School District, Parma, Ohio, USA. I'd also like to thank my editors Corinne Mooney, Charlene Nichols, and Elizabeth Hunt for their invaluable help and encouragement.

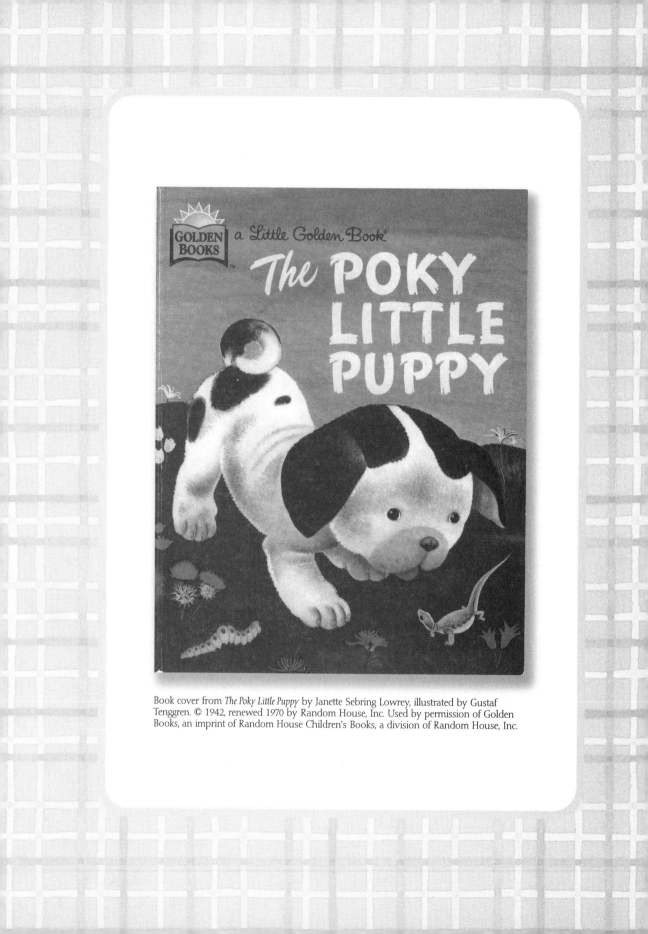

Book cover from *The Poky Little Puppy* by Janette Sebring Lowrey, illustrated by Gustaf Tenggren. © 1942, renewed 1970 by Random House, Inc. Used by permission of Golden Books, an imprint of Random House Children's Books, a division of Random House, Inc.

Chapter 1

Introduction to Books for Children

Children are never too young for you to begin developing their joy of reading by daily reading aloud to them. Some mothers even start reading to their children before they are born because there is evidence that unborn babies hear their mothers and react to their voices (see DeCasper, Lecanuet, Busnel, & Granier-Deferre, 1994).

Benefits of Reading to Children

In addition to building a bond between parents and children, daily reading to youngsters is the single most important activity for building the knowledge required for eventual success in learning to read (Anderson, Hiebert, Scott, & Wilkinson, 1985). Moreover, parents should continue to read to their children after they start school until they say they want to read on their own (or read to you).

Learning to read is a process that begins at birth when children first start to recognize speech sounds and the meanings the sounds represent. Later, children associate these sounds with the letters and letter clusters within words, and they learn how books work and how to associate pictures with words.

Children can acquire concepts, ideas, story and text structures, syntax, vocabulary, and pleasure from listening to and reading books. Each book helps children enlarge their parameters as they vicariously learn about the world and add new words to their listening, speaking, and reading vocabularies. Teachers often tell me how reading to children stimulates their imaginations and stretches their attention spans, and parents and other caregivers often remark on how it nourishes children's emotional development and strengthens bonds between children and adults.

When a young child sits in an adult's lap and they look at a picture book together (aptly called lap reading), the adult can talk about things they read and ask questions to elicit the child's oral language development. Together the child and adult can point to and discuss items in the illustrations, which provide rich clues to the meanings of words. When lap reading with a familiar book, occasionally encourage children to focus on the printed words.

One way to do this is to encourage children to join in on parts they recognize or remember. (Rhyming text lends itself especially well to this strategy because it is predictable.) Adults can facilitate this activity if they pause at the end of a sentence or line and allow children to finish it. If adults point under each word as children say them, this helps children to grasp the concept of word—that a written word is a string of letters bounded by spaces. Once children can match spoken words to their written counterparts, they have made an important discovery called speech-to-print match, and most children will then begin to learn to read many of these words by sight.

Another advantage of lap reading (which teachers achieve for groups of children by using oversized books called Big Books) is that children can quickly learn the English concepts of print, or the directionality of our written language: We read pages from top to bottom, lines from left to right, and books from front to back. (Not all written languages are arranged in this manner.) You can initiate this discovery with familiar books by running your finger under a line of text while you are reading it. (See chapter 2 for specific information on teaching children to read—or to read *better*.)

Children who have listened to a book several times can usually recite or paraphrase the text by looking at the illustrations because, in picture books, the illustrations as well as the text tell the story. (This practice is helpful later when children begin reading independently because they know to look at illustrations for clues to unknown words.) After children have memorized a simple book such as Bill Martin Jr's *Brown Bear, Brown Bear, What Do You See?*, adults can help them focus on the words by pointing under each as children recite it from memory. With this voice-pointing procedure, children can add these words to their sight-reading vocabulary, allowing them to recognize them in new contexts such as other books or in environmental print.

To optimize the benefits of reading to children, adults can ask questions before, during, and after sharing a book. This will more fully engage children in the story and give adults a window to children's responses to literature. It will also help children develop their sense of story structure, or knowledge of the various components of stories such as characters and setting.

Involving Children With Books

With new books, start by reading the title and showing the book cover or first illustration. Ask children to predict the book's contents by asking, "What do you think might happen in this book?" Once you start reading, you can stop occasionally and ask questions such as the following:

- What do you think this character might be thinking? What clues helped you?
- How do you think this character feels? What clues helped you?
- Why did _____ finally decide to _____?
- What was the reason for _____?
- What do you think might happen next? Why do you think so?

After finishing a book, discussing it with children will help them focus on the story (instead of primarily the illustrations), thus aiding their comprehension and enjoyment. Following are some examples of questions to ask after reading a book:

- Which of your predictions were true?
- What caused the problem of the main character?
- What words would you use to describe the way _____ acted?
- What did the main character find out at the end? What did the other characters learn?
- What does the title of the story mean to you now?
- What do you think is the most important thing the author might want you to remember about this story?

In reference to the last question, it is not necessary to ask children to find the author's moral after finishing each new book. Much of children's literature is moralistic, to the point that some adults expect all literature to teach a lesson or moral. However, most authors of excellent literature intend for their books to be pleasurable. Not all authors implant hidden messages in their stories, and even when they do, discussing it should not be the focus of the conversation. From reading broadly, children gain vicarious experiences about life, and they will gradually internalize important truths.

In addition, you should not expect children to express the same interpretation of a book that you have. Responses to literature are personal, and they will vary according to the individual's background experiences. If you expect children to express the same feelings you gained, they will be trying to guess what the right answers are, rather than responding with their individual reactions, which reflect their developmental levels and will change over time with subsequent readings of any given book.

Although this section contains general strategies for engaging children with books, I provide specific suggestions in many of the book annotations that appear in chapters 3 through 6.

Understanding Trends in Best–Selling Books

I have extensively analyzed the *Publishers Weekly* bestsellers data to determine important trends, and the question I am most frequently asked is, "Which authors have written the most bestsellers?" The author and illustrator team (also husband and wife) Stan and Jan Berenstain have overwhelmingly won this honor—40 all-time best-selling picture books at last count. Their series on the Berenstain Bears focuses on the ordinary problems most families encounter, such as the arrival of a new baby, the first day of school, kids' messy rooms, and eating too much junk food. The lessons and morals that this series promotes make it immensely popular with parents, and the antics of the amusing bear family make it enjoyable to children.

In addition, Mercer Mayer has written 28 all-time best-selling picture books in his Little Critter series. These books focus on tender relationships between the lovable Little Critter and his father, mother, grandfather, grandmother, and little sister. Rather than full plots, the books recount happy and funny events that Little Critter has with his family and friends, making them pleasurable books for teachers and parents to share with their children.

Dr. Seuss also has authored 25 all-time best-selling picture books. His Cat in the Hat books have enchanted children and adults alike for decades. Dr. Seuss's other memorable characters include Sam-I-Am, the Grinch, Yertle the Turtle, the Sneetches, and Horton the elephant who hatches an egg.

By far, the most popular genre in picture books is fantasy (Roback, Britton, & Hochman, 2001), and the majority of these have main characters that are anthropomorphic animals—that is, animals who act like people (Anderson, 2006b). Of the books that the three best-selling authors (Berenstains, Mayer, and Seuss) have produced, all are animal fantasy. In fact, the top three all-time best-selling children's books (which include both picture books and juvenile novels) identified by *Publishers Weekly*—with conglomerate sales approaching 36 million copies—are animal fantasy: *The Poky Little Puppy* by Janette Sebring Lowrey, *The Tale of Peter Rabbit* by Beatrix Potter, and *Charlotte's Web* by E.B. White.

Recognizing Different Picture Book Formats

Young children initially believe that the illustrations, rather than the printed words, tell the story. When you read to them, they imagine that you are telling a story from the pictures. Indeed, a good picture book does tell much of the story through its art, and children should be encouraged to look back at the pictures and retell the story when you are finished reading.

Picture books convey their messages through a series of pictures with only a small amount of text (or none at all in the case of wordless picture books). The illustrations are as important as—or more important than—the text in conveying the author's message.

Picture storybooks are picture books with a plot, meaning that the main character has a problem, sets a goal to overcome it, makes attempts to reach the goal, and finally reaches a resolution of the problem. In picture storybooks, the text and illustrations equally convey the storyline. Most people simply call these picture books as well without making the distinction of whether the book has a plot. In fact, *picture book* is an umbrella term we commonly use to refer to any book that has more illustrations than text.

Picture books of all kinds are easy to recognize because of their size and length. The pages are usually larger than in juvenile novels (which have few or no illustrations), and their shapes are more varied. The number of pages is somewhat uniform because the majority of picture books (excluding special formats such as board books and pop-up books) contain 32 pages. Longer picture books are 48 or 64 pages. (The length of most books is a multiple of 16 because of the way presses print the paper.) Each book description in the following chapters has page numbers included because the number of pages is often an indication of the age appropriateness for the book. Shorter books generally target younger children, and books become increasingly longer as the age of their targeted audience increases.

Hardcover Books

When purchasing picture books, format is an important consideration. By format, I mean the physical makeup of a book, such as the quality of binding and paper. Hardcover editions are the highest quality and most durable books, and their quality of paper ensures the best color reproduction of illustrations. Publishers construct covers with heavy cardboard that is laminated with attractive glossy paper. The pages are sewn together and held inside the book by sturdy, attractively decorated endpapers that are glued to the front and back covers.

Hardcover is the best format for books that children are going to read repeatedly. For those who want their books to last many years, I suggest buying books with library binding when available, because this is the sturdiest format of hardcover books—made to hold up through many readings by library patrons.

Paperback Books

Publishers first issue most books in hardcover. When sales slow down, they issue the books in paperback to reach a new market of buyers looking for less costly books. Usually the pages of paperback books consist of somewhat lower quality paper, and instead of being sewn, the pages are glued together and then glued to a stiff paper cover. You can identify the better made paperback books because they have a spine. That is, when placed on the shelf, you can see the back edge of the book where the title and names of author, illustrator, and publisher are printed. Paperback books are good for teachers and parents who want to build their book collections economically.

Several popular book clubs such as Carnival, Scholastic, Troll, and Trumpet market their books in schools where classroom teachers distribute the order forms to their students. Book club editions are the least costly because they are mass-produced. Quality of paper diminishes with the price, and the colors in illustrations are not always true to the originals. In addition, mass-market editions are usually stapled in the center, rather than being glued with a spine, and they are frequently smaller than regular paperbacks. However, book clubs have made great books available and affordable for nearly all children.

Board Books

In recent years, the field of early literacy has been thrust into the spotlight with a focus on promoting young children's school readiness. The research that has resulted from this focus indicates, "If children acquire certain knowledge, skills, and dispositions during the preschool years, they are likely to become successful readers and writers in the elementary grades" (Vukelich & Christie, 2004, p. 2).

The importance of parent involvement in children's preschool education has long been documented by research (Morrow, 2005). I suggest parents start with books made especially for the very young because little ones not only love to look at books—they also like to gnaw on covers, pull on pages, and toss books across the room. Therefore, in addition to being entertaining, first books for children must be very sturdy—especially if children are teething!

Both the content and format of board books are specifically designed for infants and toddlers. They typically consist of only 14 to 28 pages made of sturdy cardboard with a glossy, wipe-off finish. These durable books can range in size from 3 to 12 inches square—all with rounded corners to prevent a poke in the eye. Each page is usually illustrated with a simple picture and includes no more than a one-sentence caption. Some have only a single word under each illustration.

Few board books contain a full plot. For example, the top-selling board book *Goodnight Moon* by Margaret Wise Brown has two characters—the little bunny and the quiet old lady. It has a memorable setting in the bunny's darkening bedroom. The book even has events, such as the bunny's saying goodnight to all the familiar things in his room. However, the book does not contain a problem, conflict, or tension that is necessary for a plot. Quite the contrary, the reader becomes enmeshed in the peaceful, warm setting as the bunny goes through his nightly bedtime ritual.

Instead of telling a story, the majority of board books are concept oriented. The most popular topics include the alphabet, animals, colors, numbers, shapes, textures, and simple vocabulary such as opposites. Chapter 3 features books for children from birth through age 2, most of which are board books.

Easy-to-Read Books

If you selected 100 picture storybooks at random and reviewed each for the length and complexity of its sentences, along with word length and difficulty, you would see that generally these books are more appropriate for reading *to* young children rather than *by* young children. However, one category of picture storybooks is specifically designed to give beginning readers successful independent reading experiences. The generic name for this category is easy-to-read books, but publishers may use a variety of names, for example, I Can Read and Ready to Read books.

The distinctive features of easy-to-read books makes them easier to recognize. First, because emergent readers read them independently, the books are smaller for little hands to hold. In addition, the pages look very different from other picture books. The illustrations are designed to give clues to the meaning of the text, but the pictures are fewer and smaller. The pages contain a liberal amount of white space, achieved by larger print, more space between lines, and lines that do not run all the way to the right margin.

However, the most significant characteristic of easy-to-read books is limited vocabulary. Usually fewer than 250 different words appear in a book, and they are arranged in short, simple sentences, often with word patterns, repeated text, and even rhyming lines to make reading new words easier. The difficulty of the vocabulary is also controlled; the majority consists of single-syllable words, which are common to children's listening and speaking vocabularies. Authors of easy-to-read books often present them in several stories or short episodic chapters and include a table of contents of their titles.

The first easy-to-read book was Dr. Seuss's *The Cat in the Hat*, published in 1957. Else Holmelund Minarik's *Little Bear* followed the same year. The good stories, simple text, and delightful illustrations of these books have made them appealing to beginning readers for nearly 50 years.

Anthologies

Anthologies include a number of popular picture books, and they sell for far less than the individual books would if purchased separately. However, anthologies do have some disadvantages. Most of them are large and heavy, which makes it difficult for young children to view them independently. In addition, publishers often omit or reduce the size of illustrations to keep the volumes from being even heavier. (For example, four original book illustrations are often depicted on one anthology page.) Another limitation of some anthologies is that publishers often include only books that have been published by their company, thereby severely limiting their selections. Nonetheless, anthologies are a quick and relatively inexpensive way of building your personal collection of great picture books.

HarperCollins publishes a best-selling anthology of picture books with 12 enduring stories (*HarperCollins Treasury of Picture Book Classics: A Child's First Collection*, 2002). Unlike other anthologies, this 440-page volume preserves the feel of the originals by including all illustrations. (The trade-off is that the book is lengthy but only contains a dozen stories.) Included are stories by Russell Hoban, John Steptoe, Esphyr Slobodkina, Tomi Ungerer, Eric Carle, William Joyce, Margaret Wise Brown, Crockett Johnson, Laura Joffe Numeroff, Robert Kraus, William Steig, and Charlotte Zolotow. Following each story are comments by the editors, which include suggestions for sharing the books with children and brief biographies of the authors and illustrators.

Another popular anthology is *The Random House Book of Easy-to-Read Stories* (1993), which contains the full content and illustrations of 4 books by Dr. Seuss and 12 other popular picture books by such beloved authors and illustrators as Marc Brown, Tomie dePaola, P.D. Eastman, and Deborah Hautzig.

The 20th Century Children's Book Treasury (Knopf, 1998) is another great anthology, edited by Janet Schulman, who compiled 44 classic stories that she believed were the best published (by a variety of publishing houses) in the last century. Featured authors and illustrators include Virginia Lee Burton, Janell Cannon, Lois Ehlert, Pat Hutchins, Ezra Jack Keats, Leo Lionni, Arnold Lobel, Maurice Sendak, and Judith Viorst.

Merchandise Books

Merchandise books, sometimes called grocery store books because of where they were originally marketed (though they are now also available in drug stores, large discount chain stores, and Internet bookstores), are books with cartoon, comic book, movie, and television characters. These books are less likely to be sold in bookstores or found in public and school libraries because their primary purpose is to sell something—foods, movie tickets, dolls and toys, backpacks, admission to theme parks, and countless other things advertised on cartoon and other television shows, including breakfast cereal in the case of Lee Wade's *The Cheerios Play Book*.

These books often sell well when first published, and they sometimes appear on *weekly* bestseller lists—most likely because they are so readily accessible. The majority of families have a parent who goes shopping weekly at the grocery or discount store, and the books are relatively inexpensive—partly because of the manner in which they are constructed, but often because of the mediocre quality of their content, with text and illustrations by little known authors and illustrators. In fact, many publishers of merchandise books do not bother to include the names of the author and illustrator on their book covers.

Merchandise books appeal to young children because their characters are familiar faces from Saturday morning cartoon shows or the latest children's movie. However, I have not included any merchandise books in the following chapters for several reasons:

- I believe children are bombarded with enough advertisements by watching television and do not need to encounter them through picture books as well.
- Parents are already quite familiar with these books and do not need to read my book to learn about them.
- These books usually go out of print when the merchandise is no longer a fad; for example, *ET: The Extra-Terrestrial Storybook* by William Kotzwinkle sold more than 1.3 million copies but is long out of print.
- The purpose of my book is to promote quality literature, and few merchandise books fall in this category, which is why they go out of print so quickly.

In the case of merchandise books, sales records alone are not reliable indicators of a book's literary value. They are often just a measure of children's and parents' familiarity with the main characters. In her summary of meta-analyses of early childhood literacy research, Roskos (2005) reported, "Book quality may be more decisive in literacy learning outcomes of storybook reading than we previously thought. This suggests that we need to focus on the book itself as a scaffold to support children's literacy development" (p. 19). In order to ensure that children are more likely to have experiences with quality books, you will not find merchandise books in the following chapters.

Obtaining Books for Children

I mentioned earlier that school book clubs are a great way to build a personal library. However, you do not need to purchase all the books you share with children. All public libraries have a section devoted to children's books, and picture books are located in the E section, sorted alphabetically by the author's last name.

If you choose to purchase books, do not think they have to be new books. Yard sales, library sales, and thrift shops are great places to find good books at bargain prices. You can also find great books—both used and new—on eBay (http://www.ebay.com) and other online auction websites at reduced prices, even when you factor in shipping costs. Also, consider asking your family and friends to give you gift certificates to bookstores for birthdays and holidays.

Using This Book

In chapters 3–6, you will read about picture books, which I have grouped into four categories based on *suggested* ages when you might first introduce them: infants and ages 1–2, ages 3–4, ages 5–6, and ages 7–8. I stress that these groupings are suggestions only—children may still enjoy books that I have suggested for younger children, and they might be ready for books that I have suggested for older children. Moreover, they will certainly want to experience their favorite books repeatedly, regardless of their ages. Then, when they learn to read on their own, they will enjoy reading their older books independently or, better yet, read them to a younger sibling.

I provide the age levels for two reasons. First, I am frequently asked which books are appropriate for certain age groups. Although I generally discourage people from trying to pigeonhole books into age-appropriate groups, I recognize that many people would like to have some broad guidelines. In addition, if parents use my book when their children are young, and if their goal is to read all 200 picture books to them, these age groupings will allow parents to achieve this. By reading only two of these books a month to their children, they can enjoy them all before their children reach age 9.

However, you may find it more convenient to locate books by reviewing the subject index. Within each chapter, I have grouped books by themes, for example, *animal fantasy* and *love*, and you can use the subject index to find all the books on a particular theme. In addition, when you discover that children love a certain author or illustrator, you may wish to use the name and title index to find all the books that I have included by a particular person, which may appear in multiple chapters and themes.

Book cover from *The Real Mother Goose* by Blanche Fisher Wright, © 1916 by Scholastic.

Chapter 2

Teaching Children to Read With Literature

Reading has many definitions, but I believe this one is easiest to understand: Reading is the process of obtaining meaning from print in an interaction between the reader and written language, in which the reader reconstructs a message from the writer (Harris & Hodges, 1995). Children learn to read in an emerging process that needs to be nurtured from birth (Botzakis & Malloy, 2006) by all their caregivers: parents, grandparents, babysitters, older siblings, day-care workers, teachers, librarians, and teacher assistants.

In 2004, the Institute of Educational Sciences convened the National Early Literacy Panel. After an extensive review of research, the panel identified five characteristics of children (birth–age 5) that are most closely linked to later achievement in literacy (Strickland & Shanahan, 2004). These characteristics are as follows:

1. **oral language development**—speaking vocabulary
2. **phonological/phonemic awareness**—awareness of the sounds that make up spoken words
3. **alphabetic knowledge**—recognizing the letters that represent speech sounds
4. **print knowledge**—the conventions of a written language, including directionality
5. **invented spelling**—ability to spell words the way they sound

Children's books provide a natural medium for fostering and developing children's understanding of these critical areas, and books can also be used to assess children's progress as emergent readers. In this chapter, I explain how to use literature to develop and assess four essential components of emergent literacy:

1. letter–name and letter–sound correspondence (alphabetic knowledge, phonemic awareness, and invented spelling)

2. concepts of print (print knowledge)

3. concept of word and speech-to-print match (print knowledge, phonological awareness)

4. sense of story structure (oral language development and listening comprehension)

At the end of this chapter is an explanation of a routine you can use to teach children to read—or to read better—by devoting only 30 minutes a day.

Letter–Name and Letter–Sound Correspondence

Although many teachers and parents tell children a particular letter *makes* a sound (for example, "*d* says *duh*"), children need to internalize the principle that letters (and letter groups, such as *th* in *the*) represent the sounds of our language, and that these letters have unique names and configurations. If carefully selected, alphabet books (see chapters 3 and 4) are excellent tools for learning these concepts. Even though uppercase (capital) letters are often taught first, especially by parents, about 90% of the text that children will encounter in print consists of lowercase (small) letters, so it is actually more desirable for children to learn the lowercase letters first. Among the most useful books are those depicting the letters in both uppercase letters and lowercase letters, such as *Baby's ABC*. Also very useful are books that depict that some letters commonly represent more than one sound, such as *Dr. Seuss's ABC*.

The most beneficial alphabet books have illustrations that present familiar items that children can name. While children may not know the names of each item before you read the book to them, it is important that they recognize the items and can learn to say their names. A book that depicts an anvil for the letter *a*, for example, would be of limited benefit on independent viewings by children who have never seen an anvil and cannot remember its name.

In addition, the name of each item should begin with a phoneme (an individual sound in the English language) that is commonly represented by the featured letter, for example, "*c* is for *cat*." In some alphabet books, children are required to match a letter with a phoneme at the end or even middle of a word, for example, "*x* is for *fox*." Because beginning readers acquire the ability to isolate initial phonemes before they are able to isolate ending and middle phonemes, the latter example would be meaningless to emergent readers.

Repeated exposure to alphabet books allows children to learn not only the name and configurations for each letter but also the sounds the letter commonly represents. Once a book becomes familiar, adults can then use it informally to assess children's understanding of these concepts. For example, after reading the page about a letter, and the child has named the items illustrated, ask the child to supply another word (not shown in the illustrations) that begins with the same sound. This will give the child practice in mentally isolating the initial sounds of familiar words. This ability becomes important later as children attempt to decode unfamiliar words.

When reading a familiar alphabet book, instead of reading the text, cover the illustrations with your hand or with paper, and ask the child to name the letter and then tell you a word that begins with the sound that the letter represents. To determine if the child truly recognizes each letter—rather than the order of the letters—do this back to front and then in random order in the alphabet book.

Complete a final assessment with the Letter-Recognition Inventory on the following pages. Note that this inventory includes the alternate manuscript forms of the letters *a* and *g* because this is how children will most likely encounter them in handwritten text. In addition to checking a child's letter-name correspondence, you can also use this inventory to check a child's letter-sound correspondence: Ask the child to name a word that begins with each letter's sound. Any word beginning with the appropriate sound (but not necessarily spelled with that letter) should be considered a correct answer. For example, a response of *city* for the letter *s* is correct because the sound at the beginning of *city* is the same as the beginning of *silly*. It is critical to resist the urge to have the child conform to conventional spellings because invented spelling—spelling words the way they sound—is one of the five early characteristics of successful readers identified by the National Early Literacy Panel.

Letter–Recognition Inventory

Purposes

1. To determine whether a child can identify all the letters of the alphabet, both upper- and lowercase

2. To determine whether a child can name a word whose beginning sound is commonly represented with a certain letter

Materials

Two copies of the inventory on the next page

Procedures

1. Sit across from the child, and with the child looking at one copy of the inventory, proceed from left to right across the line, pointing to each letter and asking the child what it is. Circle unknown letters on your copy of the inventory and indicate misidentified letters by writing the child's response above it.

2. Once the child can name all of the more common letters, point to a letter and ask the child to name any word that begins with the *sound* of that letter. (Limit this to about eight or nine letters per sitting to avoid making the task too arduous.) Initially, you may need to give one or two examples, especially for letters that commonly represent more than one sound, such as the consonants *c, g, x, y* and the vowels *a, e, i, o, u.*

Interpretations

1. Many beginning readers will have difficulty recognizing *q, v,* and *z* and perhaps one or two other letters encountered out of sequence. They may also have difficulty with *b, d, g, p,* and *q* because of directional confusion with letter formation. Children who are unable to identify all the letters need additional experience with alphabet books.

2. Beginning readers are not likely to provide an appropriate word for each letter, even when spaced over three sittings. However, following the procedures outlined in the section "Letter-Name and Letter-Sound Correspondence," children should eventually be able to name words for all except the least common letters, such as *q, v, x,* and *z.* It is critical to remember that children should be encouraged, rather than corrected, if they provide a word with an appropriate beginning sound that is spelled with a different letter. For example, with the letter *g,* both *giraffe* and *jack* are appropriate responses.

(continued)

Letter-Recognition Inventory (continued)

d f t g n b e h l v o y m a

a r c q z u s j p i x k w g

F W D T N R A C G Z B Q E

V J O I Y P M X K H L S U

Concepts of Print

Initially, young children believe that the reader is telling the story in a picture book, much like a favorite bedtime story, but with the addition of visual prompts. This is evident when children, ready to view the next illustration, turn the page before you have finished reading it. Children need to understand that the print, rather than the pictures, carries the meaning of the text, and that unlike a bedtime story, it is fixed and does not vary from one reading to the next (unless you are tired of a book and attempt to condense it, which children will almost never let you get away with). Other concepts of print (directionality) in the English language that children must acquire include the following:

- Books are read from front to back.
- A page is read from top to bottom.
- A line is read from left to right.

In addition to visually recognizing these directional arrangements, children also need to comprehend the reading terminology *beginning, end, front, back, top, bottom, letter, word, line,* and *page*. Therefore, it is important to discuss books and ask questions about the illustrations and text using this terminology. For example, say, "Look at the size of the moon at the *top* of this *page*."

The first time you share a new book, allow the child to examine illustrations thoroughly before reading the text on that page. During subsequent readings, point underneath each word as you say it while reading with a normal rate and good intonation. Young children who have frequently experienced viewing a book while the reader is simultaneously tracking the print with a finger will usually acquire the concepts of print unconsciously. Books that contain illustrations on one page and text on the facing page, or have all the text at the bottom of the page—for example, *Where the Wild Things Are*—lend themselves well to this activity because children may be annoyed by a hand or arm that obstructs the illustrations.

Once children are familiar with a book, you can occasionally pause to let them supply a word. This will encourage them to track words with their eyes to spot familiar print. In this way, children can acquire an understanding of the directional arrangement of print on a page (left to right and top to bottom).

To check a child's understanding of the concepts of print, select a picture book that the child has never seen (Clay, 1979). Begin by handing the book to the child with the spine facing him or her, and say, "Show me the front of the book."

Next, open the book to a place with text on one page and an illustration on the facing page and say, "Show me where I begin reading." Note if the child points to the print (rather than the picture). If so, then note if the child is pointing to the upper left-hand corner of the page or elsewhere.

Then say, "Show me with your finger where I go next," and "Where do I go from there?" A child who understands the directional orientation of print will sweep a finger from left to right across the line and then drop to the beginning of the next line and repeat the motion.

Hand the child two small squares of blank paper, and say, "Put these on the page so that just one *word* shows between them," and then, "Now move them so that two *words* show between them." This should be repeated substituting *letter* for *word*. An incorrect response to any of these directions indicates concepts of print that need to be developed in future book–sharing sessions. In this way, the assessment is not only diagnostic, but it also presents opportunities for instruction. You can use the Concepts of Print Inventory on the following pages to record children's knowledge of print orientation.

Concepts of Print Inventory

Purpose
To assess a child's orientation to books and written language

Materials
A simple illustrated children's book (that the child has not seen before) and two small pieces of blank paper (about one inch square)

Procedure
Hand the child the book with the spine facing him or her, and give directions on the following page, providing ample time for the child to respond.

Interpretation
Using the record sheet on the following page, put a check by the print orientation concepts that the child demonstrates. Very young children may demonstrate little or no understanding of these concepts. However, this inventory should be used to determine just which concepts the child lacks so these can be reinforced during shared reading and reassessed later. Before entering kindergarten, it is important for children to know all the concepts, so any that are still lacking should be demonstrated and then followed with reinforcement during book sharing.

(continued)

Concepts of Print Inventory (continued)

1. Knowledge of the layout of books:
   "Show me the front of the book."

2. Knowledge that we read print, not pictures:
   "Show me where I begin reading."

3. Directional orientation of print on the page:
   "Show me with your finger where I go next."
   "Where do I go from there?"

4. Knowledge of the concepts *beginning* and *end*:
   "Point to the beginning of the story on this page."
   "Point to the end of the story on this page."

5. Knowledge of the terms *top* and *bottom*:
   "Show me the bottom of the page."
   "Show me the top of the page."
   "Show me the top of the picture."
   "Show me the bottom of the picture."

6. Knowledge of the terms *word* and *letter*:
   "Put these cards on the page, so that just one *word* shows between them.
      them.
   "Now move them, so that two *words* show between them."
   "Now move them again, so that one *letter* shows between them."
   "Now move them, so that two *letters* show between them."

Concept of Word and Speech–to–Print Match

Many children confuse the concepts of *letter*, *word*, and *line*. For example, in the preceding assessment, a child might show the examiner two letters instead of two words, or one line instead of one word. Children must have a well-developed concept of word before formal reading and writing instruction can be effective. First, they must be able mentally to separate individual words in spoken language. Next, they must understand that each spoken word has a written counterpart that is a string of letters bounded by a blank space on each end.

Children can acquire these concepts when you use the voice-pointing procedure. This works best with a familiar book that has simple, repetitive text, such as *Brown Bear, Brown Bear, What Do You See?* After a few readings, most children can recite the text of this book, prompted by the illustrations. Move the child's pointing finger under each word as the child recites the text, being careful to make an exact speech-to-print match. If the child is reciting too rapidly, it may be necessary to read the text together at a slower pace. Then, the child should practice this voice-pointing procedure independently, moving his or her own finger.

You may also use the voice-pointing procedure to assess the child's ability to identify words as written units in print. For assessment, it is necessary to use a book that is new to the child but has familiar text, such as *Mary Had a Little Lamb* by Sarah Josepha Hale. Before introducing the book, ensure that the child can recite the first four lines word for word. Next, allow the child to examine the illustrations while sitting beside you. Then, you read the first four lines (only once), pointing *under* each word as you say it at a normal pace, while the child observes. (It is critical that the finger is under the word and not on top of it, obstructing the child's view.) Last, pass the book to the child and ask him or her to do the same.

Observe whether the child is able to achieve an exact speech-to-print match and can self-correct when the spoken and written words do not match. A child who points to *letters* for *words* or *words* for *syllables* needs more experience with this activity. Use the Speech-to-Print Match Inventory on the following pages to record children's ability to make a speech-to-print match with a simple nursery rhyme.

Speech–to–Print Match Inventory

Purpose
To determine the child's concept of word and ability to match spoken words with their written counterparts

Materials
Two copies of the following page

Procedures
1. Before showing the poem in print, recite the four lines until the child has memorized them.
2. Seat the child next to you and, using the printed poem, read the lines aloud while you point under each word.
3. Without help, have the child recite the lines and point under each word as he or she says it.
4. Carefully observe the child to see if he or she is achieving speech-to-print match by pointing to each word as it is said. If so, then call out the words, one at a time in random order, and ask the child to point to each in the poem.

Interpretation
Children who have a well-developed concept of word are able to voice-point with near perfection, correcting their own errors when necessary. Children who do not perform in this manner need continued practice with the read-and-point routine.

(continued)

Speech–to–Print Match Inventory (continued)

Humpty Dumpty sat on a wall.

Humpty Dumpty had a great fall.

All the king's horses and all the king's men

Could not put Humpty together again.

Sense of Story Structure

In order to comprehend stories—first by listening and later by reading—children must develop an understanding for the way stories are structured. All stories have a beginning in which the author introduces the characters, setting, problem, and goal to overcome the problem; a middle that consists of several attempts to overcome the problem (or several events that lead to the solution); and an ending in which the problem is resolved. Children need numerous opportunities to listen to literature for their sense of story structure to develop.

When a child listens to a book for the first time, I suggest using the Listening Prediction Activity on the following page to assess a child's sense of story structure, providing the book has a strong plot. First, read the title and allow the child to study the cover or first illustration. Then ask the child, "What might happen in this story?" After the child makes the first prediction, read the story, stopping two or three times (just before something important happens) to ask, "What do you think might happen next?" You may ask the child to back up a prediction by probing with the question, "Why do you think so?"

A child with a well-developed sense of story structure will be able to make logical predictions based on prior events in the story and on his or her own life experiences. *Frog and Toad Together* and the other books in this series lend themselves especially well to this activity. See the Listening Prediction Activity for questions to ask yourself during this assessment.

You should use the Listening Prediction Activity only the *first* time the child hears a particular story. In later readings, you may occasionally wish to use an oral retelling to check the child's developing sense of story structure and to encourage his or her development of oral language. After finishing a familiar book, ask the child to retell the story as if he or she were telling it to a friend who had never heard it before. Check off each of the components of story structure that the child mentions, using the items in the Story Retelling Strategy on page 27.

You may probe the child's responses by asking, "What else do you remember?" However, do not prompt with specific items, such as, "Who was the main character?" Otherwise, this becomes a simple question-and-answer session. Children's retelling of any particular story should become increasingly complex over time. Both the Listening Prediction Activity and the Story Retelling Strategy develop, as well as assess, a child's sense of story structure. I suggest you use them frequently as part of your book sharing experiences with emerging readers. However, it is very important to keep in mind that the primary purpose of reading to children is for their enjoyment.

Listening Prediction Activity

Purpose

To determine whether a child can predict what might happen next in a story, based on his or her understanding of story structure

Materials

A picture book with a well-developed plot that the child has *not* heard before

Procedure

Read the child the title of the book and let him or her look at the book cover or first illustration. Ask the child what he or she thinks might happen in this story. Read the story aloud in parts, pausing two or three times just *before* some important event, and ask the child to predict what he or she thinks might happen next in the story.

> Questions to Ask
>
> • From hearing the title and looking at the cover/first illustration, what do you think might happen in this story?
>
> • Why do you think so?
>
> • What do you think might happen next?
>
> • Why do you think so? (Repeat the last two questions after appropriate stops.)

Interpretation

To determine whether the child has a well-developed sense of story structure and adequate oral language to express it, ask yourself the following questions:

> • Was the child able to detect clues from the title and book cover illustration?
>
> • Did the child look for information from the pictures?
>
> • Are the child's story predictions wild and random, or are they based on prior incidents in the story and on what might happen in real life?
>
> • Can the child give reasons for his or her predictions?

Children who do not demonstrate an understanding of story structure need more experience listening to stories with strong plots, followed by discussion of the various story elements (see the Story Retelling Strategy).

What Should I Read Aloud? A Guide to 200 Best-Selling Picture Books by Nancy A. Anderson. © 2007 Nancy A. Anderson, Inc. Published by the International Reading Association. May be copied for classroom use.

Story Retelling Strategy

Characters:

    1.

    2.

    3.

Setting:

    Where

    When

Problem main character encountered:

Goal to overcome problem:

Attempts to reach goal or events leading to resolution:

    1.

    2.

    3.

Resolution of problem:

Thirty–Minute Nightly Routine

If a child indicates good development of the five essential components of emergent literacy described in this chapter, you can help him or her learn to read independently by devoting about 30 minutes a day.

Part I: Read to the Child (10 minutes)
Read to the child six nights a week from a book he or she is not able to read independently but can understand when you read it aloud. When reading a book for the first time, ask prediction questions: for example, "From looking at the cover (or first illustration) and listening to the title, what do you think might happen in this story?" After reading a few pages ask, "What do you think might happen next?" Repeat this question every few pages and let the child predict what might happen next in the story. You can only ask prediction questions with new books. (Otherwise, they would be memory recall questions.) After reading a familiar book, ask the child to retell the story as if he or she were telling it to a friend who had never heard it before. Spend about 10 minutes reading to the child at the beginning of each session.

On the seventh night, have the child dictate an account of something he or she has experienced, such as a trip to the park, movie, favorite television show, visit from a relative, family pet, something done with a friend, or something that happened at school. Write each sentence after the child dictates it. When the child has finished dictating, read the whole paragraph back, pointing under each word as you say it. Next, have the child read it with you. Then have the child read it alone. This is called a language experience account (LEA).

Part II: Listen to the Child Read (15 minutes)
Listen to the child read from an easy, familiar book. (If the child is a beginning reader, you may wish to start with the easy-to-read books described in the first part of chapter 5.) As the child is reading, take care not to correct every error. If an error does not change the meaning, ignore it, and let the child continue. However, if the error does change the meaning, wait until the child reads to the end of the sentence to see if he or she will go back and self-correct. If not, ask the child to stop, and then you read the sentence exactly the way he or she did. For example, if the child substitutes the word *green* for the word *great* and does not self-correct by the end of the sentence, say, "Wait a minute. Let me read that sentence to you the way you read it to me: 'Trigger was a green horse.' Does that make sense?" Point to the word missed, and ask the child to think of another word that would make sense in the sentence. This will help the child develop use of context clues for decoding unknown words.

When the child is reading and comes to an unknown word, wait at least five seconds to see if he or she can figure it out from the context and the way the word is spelled. (I suggest slowly counting to 5 to resist the urge to blurt it out.) If the child does not say the word correctly after five seconds, tell it to him or her and let the child

(continued)

continue to read. Avoid saying, "Sound it out." This discourages the child from using context to help decode unknown words. If the child is able to sound out the word, he or she will do so without your prompting, which actually distracts the child from thinking.

With beginning readers or reluctant readers, use the following support reading strategies with easy-to-read or repetitive books (sometimes called pattern books), such as *The Napping House*.

- Echo Reading. You read a sentence (or line) while pointing under each word. Next, the child reads the same sentence (or line) while pointing.
- Choral Reading. You and the child read the story together as you set the pace and model good intonation.
- Paired Reading. Sit with the child to your right. You read the left-hand pages of the book, and the child reads the right-hand pages. Switch sides and reread the book.

Spend about 15 minutes listening to the child read each session.

Part III: Review (5 minutes)

Construct a word bank of sight words the child has mastered from books and LEAs. Write these on small note cards and store them alphabetically in a file box. Spend the last five minutes of each session rereading LEAs (six nights a week) or reviewing the words in the word bank (one night a week).

If you are loyal in devoting 30 minutes a night (the time it takes to watch a television rerun) in reading with the child, you can greatly enhance his or her reading ability. Following is a quick summary of this easy routine.

Nightly Routine Summary

- For the first 10 minutes, read a new book to the child and ask prediction questions (six nights a week), or write a language experience account (LEA) once a week.
- For the next 15 minutes, listen to the child read a familiar book without overcorrecting mistakes.
- For the last 5 minutes, reread previously written LEAs (six nights a week), or read all the words in the bank once a week.

Things to Remember

Avoid requiring children to pronounce accurately every word on the printed page by dwelling on decoding strategies, such as phonics. Keep in mind that the objective of reading is to obtain meaning from print, so this should always be the primary goal.

Intervene only when children request help or when children substitute a word that significantly changes the meaning of the author. Also, avoid requiring children to read everything systematically. When reading just for fun, the pace is often more rapid than when reading for comprehension. For example, children would most likely read a pattern book or a familiar book with predictable text at a faster pace than a new book.

Book cover from *Pat the Bunny* by Dorothy Kunhardt. © 1940, renewed 1968 by Penk, Inc. Used by permission of Golden Books, an imprint of Random House Children's Books, a division of Random House, Inc.

Chapter 3

Best–Selling Books for Infants and Children Ages 1–2

Children are never too young for you to read to them, and I strongly urge parents to start when their children are infants. This chapter gives you ideas for books to read to your children from birth through age 2. The majority are board books, sturdy little books that consist of about 14 to 28 thick cardboard pages with rounded corners. Sometimes picture books that sell well in hardcover and paperback editions are later published as board books (although the text is often condensed). However, most board books have been specifically designed for this format.

Rather than containing a story, board books are almost entirely concept oriented with topics such as the alphabet, animals, colors, numbers, opposites, shapes, and textures. In this chapter on books for the youngest of children, the majority (but not all) are board books specifically designed to be baby's first books.

Bedtime

Bedtime and books go together like milk and cookies. There is no better way for a parent, grandparent, or babysitter to get a child settled into bed than to pull out a favorite picture book. Then, instead of bedtime becoming something for children to dread and fight against, it becomes an enjoyable time when the caregiver and child can unwind and be close to each other. Often young children will drift off to sleep with happy characters and thoughts on their minds to dream about. As they get older, be prepared for them to negotiate for you to read "just one more book, pleeeease!"

Goodnight Moon by Margaret Wise Brown, illustrated by Clement Hurd. (1947). HarperCollins. 32 pages. The all-time best-selling board book is *Goodnight Moon* (also available in regular hardcover and paperback). Generations of children have loved this book since it was first published in 1947. Illustrations depicting an old rotary telephone and the presence of a fireplace in the bedroom indicate a specific era, but the text is timeless. In lulling language, the author gives an account of a little bunny whose green bedroom grows increasingly darker as he goes through his nightly bedtime routine of saying goodnight to his room and all the familiar things visible. Looking for all the objects the bunny names is a fun way for children to interact with this book. Sharp eyes will even spot a copy of *Goodnight Moon* on the nightstand. Especially entertaining is the little mouse, climbing around the room as the clock indicates the increasing lateness of the hour. At the end, the little bunny succumbs to slumber, secure that all the beloved things inside his room (and visible through the window) will still be there when he awakens.

The Going to Bed Book by Sandra Boynton. (1995). Little Simon. 16 pages. Author, artist, and musical composer Sandra Boynton—also known for her greeting cards—publishes extra-appealing board books with oddball humor that delight children and adults with their enchanting silliness. Her whimsical and hilarious style features zany animal characters, such as the elephant, moose, and pig in *The Going to Bed Book*. Children will see their own bedtime routines as fun when they see the animals prepare for bed by taking a bath (in one big tub), finding their pajamas, brushing their teeth, and finally rocking to sleep in the ark. The simple rhymes, goofy animals, and sweet lyrics in all of Boynton's books make for memorable reading experiences. Equally fun is her *Pajama Time!*

The Napping House by Audrey Wood, illustrated by Don Wood. (1984). Harcourt Brace Jovanovich. 32 pages. In rhythmic and repetitive text, and with illustrations in beautiful shades of blue and lavender, children experience a bedroom scene, depicting a dark and rainy day through the window. A granny is sound asleep, snoring in her cozy little bed, and her grandson, who has been nodding in a nearby chair, joins her with his pillow (right on top of Granny). The dreaming boy is followed by a dozing dog, a snoozing cat, a slumbering mouse, and a flea—but the flea has no intention of sleeping. He hops on top of the stack to take a nip out of the mouse, which causes quite a commotion.

Children will enjoy tracking the flea's progress to the top of the stack by looking for the small black dot (encircled by a halo) in each of the illustrations.

Good Night, Gorilla by Peggy Rathmann. (1994). Putnam. 32 pages. A weary—but fatherly—watchman walks by the gorilla cage, making his last nightly round at the zoo, unaware that the crafty creature has pickpocketed his keys and stealthily trails him, unlocking the cages of every animal the guard bids good night to. All animals quietly parade behind the oblivious guard as he traipses home to his nearby cottage. The animals are able to slip unnoticed into his bedroom, and the cheeky little gorilla even snuggles next to the sleepy wife as she turns out the lights. When all of the creatures reply to the wife's, "Good night, dear," they are exposed! After several readings, encourage children to make up a story about the unnamed mouse who appears in every illustration, first drifting up on a red balloon to the top of the gorilla cage to pick a banana, and then trailing the balloon behind him to, from, and then back again to the cottage bedroom for a nighttime snack.

Time for Bed by Mem Fox, illustrated by Jane Dyer. (1997). Red Wagon. 28 pages. In this gentle bedtime lullaby, darkness is falling while various affectionate animal parents get their offspring ready for a cozy sleep. In rhymed couplets and repetitive text, the narrator bids good night to each animal family as the mothers endearingly cuddle with their little ones. In the final double-page spread (two facing pages in a book), a blond-headed toddler nods off to sleep as Mother hugs him closely.

Animals

If you look back at the five bedtime books, you will notice that all of them have animal characters, most of whom act like humans—either just speaking and thinking like humans, as in *Good Night, Gorilla*, or acting entirely humanlike, as the bunny does in *Goodnight Moon*. Research indicates that animal fantasy books are young children's favorite genre (Anderson, 2006b; Lawson, 1972; Peterson, 1971). Nearly one-third of the all-time best-selling children's books published in the United States are animal fantasy (Roback, Britton, & Hochman, 2001), and more than one-third of publishers' new titles are animal fantasy (Anderson & Eitelgeorge, in press). Therefore, it is not surprising that books about animals are abundant in this chapter and the ones that follow.

Moo Baa La La La **by Sandra Boynton. (1982). Little Simon. 14 pages.** With what the publisher calls "serious silliness for all ages," artist Sandra Boynton is better than ever with completely redrawn versions of her multimillion-selling board books, the most popular of which is *Moo Baa La La La*. Whimsical and hilarious animals entertain infants with their oddball antics while making the traditional animal sounds—all except for the three dancing pigs who sing "La La La." If Boynton's art looks familiar, chances are you have seen it on one of the more than 8,000 greeting cards she designed, or on the collections of children's wallpaper, T-shirts, balloons, plush toys, stationery items, and mugs that are adorned with her artwork.

Barnyard Dance! **by Sandra Boynton. (1993). Workman. 24 pages.** This joyful book features a bespectacled fiddle-playing cow and a pig twirling a sheep at a barnyard dance. The die-cut cover (cut-out hole) frames a picture of its zany characters. The farm animals dance a boisterous, knee-slapping square dance, which the fiddle-playing cow calls in cadence. Everyone will want to sing along as the animals do-si-do in the barnyard with a baa and a moo and a cock-a-doodle-doo as everybody promenades, two by two! I also recommend *Philadelphia Chickens* for another Boynton song and dance book—this one with musical notations as well as lyrics.

Big Red Barn **by Margaret Wise Brown, illustrated by Felicity Bond. (1956). HarperFestival. 32 pages.** The beloved author of *Goodnight Moon* created another all-time favorite with *Big Red Barn*, which tells about the cycle of a day in a barnyard, where a family of animals (and the old scarecrow) peacefully play and sleep in the grass and the hay. Horses, sheep, goats, geese, chickens, cows, and a pink piglet (who is learning to squeal) cavort around the big red barn in the great green field.

Farm Animals **by Phoebe Dunn. (1984). Random House. 28 pages.** The cover illustration of an adorable pink piglet perched on a fence railing invites children to look inside this chunky little book. In lively full-color photographs, all the friendly animals on the farm—including ducks, chickens, pigs, sheep, and horses—are identified by name. Though the text is sparse, adults can provide the animal sounds and interesting information about the critters, making this a great book for lap reading.

The Farm Book by Jan Pfloog. (1968). Golden Books. 24 pages. This is not a typical farm book with just the pictures, names, and noises of animals. It also shows the everyday activities of a farm family, including two children who jump in the hayloft and hug the woolly lambs while the farmer milks the cows and feeds the sheep and turkeys—and what a horde of turkeys it is!

The Zoo Book by Jan Pfloog. (1967). Golden Books. 24 pages. An attractive baby zebra adorns the cover of this inviting book, which is a companion to Pfloog's *The Farm Book*. Teachers and parents can find great ideas on how to use this and other books with zoo themes for fun learning activities at a link from the Alphabet Soup site (http://www.thekcrew.net/zoounit.html).

The Kitten Book by Jan Pfloog. (1968). Golden Books. 24 pages. All baby animals, but especially tiny and fuzzy kittens, are attractive to children, who can relate to the animals' diminutive size, playful nature, and helplessness. With easy-to-read text and attractive drawings, little ones can learn about the life of a kitten in this slim book. On a child's level, the author explains how kittens grow up. She provides interesting information, such as kittens will open their eyes for the first time at 2 weeks of age, and they are able to lap milk from a bowl at 6 weeks. Families who are planning to get a kitten will find this a valuable introduction. In addition, children who are born into families with an existing cat can enjoy seeing what their pet might have been like when it was a baby.

Animal Babies by Harry McNaught. (1977). Random House. 14 pages. The cover of this thick board book depicts a mother red fox with her four contented little pups. Through colorful illustrations and easy-to-read text, children can learn to recognize and name 20 types of baby animals and their mothers—both domestic and wild—including a cygnet (swan), fawn (deer), foal (horse), joey (kangaroo), and kit (rabbit). Older children who have grown fond of this book might enjoy finding the names of other baby animals by searching the Utah Education Network (http://www.uen.org/utahlink/activities/view_activity.cgi?activity_id=4777).

Baby's Animal Friends by Phoebe Dunn. (1988). Random House. 28 pages. Delightful full-color photographs capture the special bond between young children and baby animals. The cover photo of a towheaded toddler kissing a baby rabbit sets the tone for these authentic photos of baby animals, along with a few baby humans as well. If you want children to see what real animals look like (as opposed to the cartoon-like drawings in many animal board books), have them view these photos of little animals, such as a sleeping fawn and a tiny lamb.

Neighborhood Animals by Marilyn Singer, illustrated by Nadeem Zaidi. (2001). Baby Einstein. 16 pages. With both colorful illustrations and real photographs, eight animals are introduced: dog, cat, bird, rabbit, mouse, ladybug, duck, and frog. Text under each illustration contains a discussion question and three facts about each animal.

Polar Bear, Polar Bear, What Do You Hear? by Bill Martin Jr, illustrated by Eric Carle. (1991). Henry Holt. 32 pages. The setting of this book is a zoo where an elephant, hippo, lion, and other animals are asked what they hear. Each answer leads to the animal on the next page, and the book culminates with a zookeeper and a group of multiracial children, each disguised as one of the animals in the book. The brief, rhythmic words are easy for children to memorize and recite as they look back at the pages. They will have fun saying the names of the animals—fluting flamingo, bellowing walrus, hissing boa constrictor, and more!

Love

One topic that needs little introduction is parents' love for their children. Three special board books allow little ones to experience security and comfort in unconditional parental adoration.

Guess How Much I Love You by Sam McBratney, illustrated by Anita Jeram. (1994). Candlewick. 20 pages. A little hare tests his father's love by declaring his own: "Guess how much I love you?" Little Nutbrown Hare says he loves Big Nutbrown Hare as far as he can reach and as high as he can hop. However, Big Nutbrown Hare loves his son as far as *his* long arms can reach and as high as *his* strong legs can hop, which is much farther. Gentle competition ensues as each avows affection in ever more expansive terms. Finally, on the edge of sleep, the son says that he loves his father right up to the moon, which is very far, but as Father kisses his son goodnight, he replies that he loves him right up to the moon—and back. The watercolor illustrations, in soft earthy tones and delicate ink-line details, beautifully capture the loving relationship between parent and child.

The Runaway Bunny by Margaret Wise Brown, illustrated by Clement Hurd. (1942). HarperFestival. 40 pages. A little rabbit who wants to run away tells his mother how he will escape, but she tells him she will run after him because he is her little bunny. Thus begins the delightful banter, and no matter how many forms the little bunny takes—a fish in a trout stream, a rock on a high mountain, a crocus in a hidden garden, or a bird flying to a tree—his protective mother finds a way of retrieving him.

Following each of the pages in which the bunny tells of his next hiding place and the mother tells how she will find him is a colorful double-page spread, illustrating their imaginary game of hide-and-seek. The most touching illustration is the bunny with large graceful wings flying to the tree whose leaves have taken the shape of mother bunny with outstretched arms. The illustrations are very dreamlike, and they give young viewers a strong sense of security. This book will comfort a child who has tested the strength of his mother's love because the mother in the story always finds a way to draw her child back into her arms and loving care.

In the bunny's final attempt to hide from his mother, he fantasizes becoming a little boy and hiding in a house. The colorful spread that follows was the inspiration for another book that Brown and Hurd published several years later. Children will enjoy comparing this page to the "Goodnight room" page in *Goodnight Moon*. They will see the same little bunny clad in blue-and-white striped pajamas, blazing fireplace, picture of the cow jumping over the moon, round table with blue and yellow lamp, and even the little mouse hiding in a corner. Likewise, in the *Goodnight Moon* page, viewers will see a scene from *The Runaway Bunny* in a picture hanging on the nursery wall.

I Love You as Much... by Laura Krauss Melmed, illustrated by Henri Sorensen. (1993). HarperFestival. 22 pages. This gentle picture book lullaby celebrates the love between mothers and children, starting with pairs (mothers and offspring) of various animals—horses, bears, camels, geese, sheep, mice, goats, and whales—in natural settings, and it ends with a young human mother and her newborn child. The poem is written in quatrains that break into couplets across each double-page spread, describing each mother's testament of love. Sorensen's watercolor illustrations extend to the edges of each page, which all have full backgrounds and panoramic views. Each mother animal's love poem to her baby appears in the corner of a page where it does not block the touching illustrations.

First Words

After an extensive review of research, the National Early Literacy Panel (Strickland & Shanahan, 2004) identified those characteristics of children from birth through age 5 that are most closely linked to later achievement in literacy, and oral language development was at the top of their list.

When children's caregivers read to them regularly, children's oral language develops more rapidly. Children are first able to listen to and understand words and phrases that they hear in conversations and in books. (This is called their listening vocabulary.) Later, children begin to speak these words, using them in appropriate context (called their speaking vocabulary). Eventually, children will match the spoken words to their written counterparts, and this is how children develop their reading vocabulary—the words they can recognize on sight. Numerous best-selling books are designed to develop young children's listening and speaking vocabularies. While children may outgrow the topics of these books, they will enjoy them anew when they learn how to read them independently or to read them to a younger sibling.

My First Word Board Book by Angela Wilkes. (1997). Disney Press. 32 pages. In this miniature visual dictionary, children view double-page spreads that contain familiar categories such as animals, bathroom items, clothing, colored shapes, food, garage items, kitchen items, numbers, moving things, and toys. Each category contains about 15 labeled photographs, which serve to present simple word concepts. In addition, the groupings help young minds to categorize objects while connecting words to their associated images. A valuable feature of this book is that each item is labeled in lowercase (small) letters only, making it easier for emergent readers to recognize the words. (At least 90% of the letters young children encounter in print are lowercase, so it is the most desirable form to learn first.)

Big Dog...Little Dog by P.D. Eastman. (1973). Random House. 32 pages. The bold, colorful drawings in this book emphasize the concept of *opposites* with humor. The book opens by explaining that Fred and Ted are two dogs who are best friends, but they are opposite in every way. For example, Fred is big but Ted is little, and Fred always has money but Ted is always broke. Unlike most concept books, this book contains episodes and action to maintain children's interest in the characters and their predicaments.

Babies by Gyo Fujikawa. (1977). Grosset & Dunlap. 14 pages. This charming first look at the sweet world of a variety of ethnically diverse babies is introduced with a cover illustration of a young boy cuddling his baby sister. Inside, infants and toddlers will learn that all babies like to be loved, hugged, and cuddled—the perfect things to do while you are reading this book. Their comparative descriptions, such as *big* and *little*, *naughty* and *nice*, *sleeping* and *waking*, and *crying* and *happy*, make this book a good introduction to the concept of opposites.

Oh My Oh My Oh Dinosaurs! by Sandra Boynton. (1993). Workman. 24 pages. The inimitable Sandra Boynton makes learning opposites fun with her sassy and energetic dinosaurs. Through activities such as singing, sunbathing, painting, dancing, and playing volleyball, a gang of personable dinosaurs demonstrates concepts such as *good* and *bad*, *happy* and *sad*, *early* and *later*, and *plump* and *lean*. A die-cut cover introduces the colorful, humorous characters.

Olivia's Opposites by Ian Falconer. (2002). Atheneum. 12 pages. Falconer's irrepressible Olivia, the rambunctious little piglet, demonstrates word pairs with a comic flair. In Falconer's signature black-and-red illustrations on a white background, Olivia acts out opposites such as *plain* and *fancy*, *loud* and *quiet*, *up* and *down*, and *long*—modeling her scarlet evening gown—and *short*—flaunting a red tutu. Though Olivia's energy seems endless (at least to her parents), the book aptly ends with the sleepy, pajama-clad Olivia and her *open* (yawning) and *closed* (finally!) mouth.

Mirror Me! by Julie Aigner-Clark, illustrated by Nadeem Zaidi. (2002). Baby Einstein. 12 pages. Parents can use this book to entertain infants and to help toddlers learn the names for parts of the face—such as *forehead*, *lips*, *ears*, *hair*, and *chin*—while looking at their own faces in the book's mirrors (thin reflective film on each spread). They will also have fun imitating faces made by the book's characters. This engaging little book offers many opportunities to interact with children.

Hand, Hand, Fingers, Thumb by Al Perkins, illustrated by Eric Gurney. (1969). Random House. 24 pages. A madcap band of dancing and prancing monkeys explain *hands*, *fingers*, and *thumb* while using their hands to beat on various drums. The strong rhythm of the text encourages children to chime in during parts they remember. Do not be surprised if they tap on something to match the rhythm of "dum ditty, dum ditty, dum dum dum."

Alphabet

In addition to oral language, the National Early Literacy Panel (Strickland & Shanahan, 2004) identified phonological/phonemic awareness and alphabet knowledge as characteristics of young children that are most closely linked to later achievement in literacy.

Alphabet books, also called ABC books, are concept books that present the letters of the alphabet. Because these books are often children's first introduction to the symbols that represent the English language, you should select them carefully. The best books present the letters in alphabetical order in both lowercase and uppercase forms.

Often, each double-page spread is devoted to one letter, and the pages contain a number of things whose labels begin with the featured letter. Encourage children to look carefully at the letter and say its name; then help them name all the things on the page, reinforcing that those words begin with the featured letter and sound. In this manner, children can learn the phonemes, or individual sounds of our language.

Chicka Chicka ABC by Bill Martin Jr and John Archambault, illustrated by Lois Ehlert. (1993). Little Simon. 14 pages. This colorful board book is great for introducing the alphabet to infants. In this rollicking little chant, all the little letters of the alphabet race up the coconut tree in a humorous game of tag. It all starts when *a* tells *b* he will meet him at the top of the coconut tree. Then *d* dares *e, f*, and *g* to beat him to the top of the coconut tree. After all the letters make it to the top, then *chicka, chicka, boom, boom,* they all fall down! This board book was adapted from the full-size hardcover edition of *Chicka Chicka Boom Boom*. Unlike most other adapted board books, the authors gave it a slightly different name so that people who are familiar with the original would not be disappointed that it was condensed to make it more appropriate for infants and toddlers, whose attention spans would not be maintained with the original 40-page version.

The Alphabet Book by P.D. Eastman. (1974). Random House. 24 pages. With comical illustrations, Eastman presents the letters of the alphabet from

American ants, birds on bikes, and cow in car, through zebras with zithers. A unique feature is the alphabet that runs down the side of each page, highlighting the letter featured on that page. Show children how to run a finger down the page, reciting the alphabet, and when they get to the highlighted letter, they will be able to reinforce the letter name with the written symbol.

Baby's ABC by Anita Shevett and Steve Shevett. (1986). Random House. 28 **pages.** This diminutive book contains 26 full-color photographs of babies and familiar objects in their world, making it very appropriate for a first alphabet book. Pages present objects of interest to toddlers, such as apples, crayons, ice cream, keys, lollipops, rattles, telephones, wagons, and zippers in an uncluttered manner on bright backgrounds. Each page contains the featured letter in both lower- and uppercase.

A to Z by Sandra Boynton. (1984). Little Simon. 10 pages. Printed on thick board pages, this book presents a variety of humorous animal characters that introduce the letters of the alphabet. As in Boynton's other whimsical and hilarious books, animals such as aardvarks, beavers, cats, and zebras cavort around the pages to the delight of young viewers who are learning while being entertained.

Colors

Another popular topic for concept books is color, and authors and illustrators have imaginative ways to introduce the basic colors, including primary (red, yellow, and blue), secondary (orange, green, and purple), and tertiary (vermilion, marigold, chartreuse, aquamarine, violet, and magenta).

Blue Hat, Green Hat by Sandra Boynton. (1984). Little Simon. 14 **pages.** Ridiculous and loveable animals introduce both the basic colors and familiar items of clothing. The elephant, bear, moose, and turkey appear in a variety of colorful, silly attire. The turkey has two fewer legs than the other characters, so he always ends up wearing the clothing in some strange manner (for example, a shirt around his tail feathers). The other animals are far from static, such as on the page where the elephant, bear, and moose are standing on their hands while wearing colored pants. To make learning the colors a little more challenging, each sequence has the colors in a different order to ensure that children are really recognizing them and not just memorizing the order.

Brown Bear, Brown Bear, What Do You See? by Bill Martin Jr, illustrated by Eric Carle. (1996). Henry Holt. 32 pages. This board book is a revised version of the classic 1983 hardcover edition (now out of print). Martin's gentle rhythmic repetition, and Carle's gorgeous, tissue-paper collage (a technique of cutting or tearing paper or fabric shapes that are assembled and glued on a surface) illustrations introduce children to a menagerie of colorful animals, who—on each double-page spread—nudge the reader onward to discover the next creature. The colorful illustrations of the brown bear, red bird, yellow duck, blue horse, green frog, purple cat, white dog, black sheep, and goldfish reinforce both color and animal concepts. This new edition has stronger colors and texture that delineate animal bodies more sharply. In addition, Carle slightly changed the positions and shapes of the animals from the original, resulting in a more energized look. Because the text is composed of only 32 different words, this makes a great first reader for children (also available in both hardcover and paperback editions).

Good Night, Sweet Butterflies: A Color Dreamland by Dawn Bentley, illustrated by Heather Cahoon. (2003). Little Simon. 24 pages. Nine sparkly, three-dimensional butterflies (covered with glitter) flit through color-themed pages that offer a place for the little butterflies to sleep. Vibrantly colorful flowers, birds, and insects adorn each illustration. Thick pages make it easy to turn (and harder to tear). The final page reunites all the butterflies and colorful animals, and invites children to say goodnight to them all. The butterflies are securely mounted, but it is still possible for children to remove one, so young children should not be allowed to view this book independently to avoid a choking hazard.

Numbers

Children are at an advantage if they enter kindergarten knowing the counting numbers 1–10, and the following books will make learning these essential concepts fun.

Five Little Monkeys Jumping on the Bed by Eileen Christelow. (1989). Clarion Books. 14 pages. You may remember the catchy finger play from your childhood: "Five little monkeys, jumping on the bed; one fell off and bumped his head." Eileen Christelow retells this delightful old counting rhyme in a charming picture book with her amusing colored-pencil drawings of the rambunctious siblings. In this cumulative verse, children learn to count backward from 5 to 1 with the five silly monkeys who insist on bedtime mayhem, regardless of the doctor's admonition after each in turn suffers the same injury. Finally, all the weary monkey children are asleep, albeit with bandaged heads, and Mother can go to bed. At the end, we discover where the children learned their bed-jumping skills. This also makes for good bedtime reading because it begins with the little monkeys' nighttime routine of taking a bath, putting on pajamas, brushing teeth, and being tucked in. However, before you leave the room, you will want to stress, *"No little monkey jumping on the bed!"*

***Olivia Counts* by Ian Falconer. (2002). Atheneum. 12 pages.** *Olivia Counts* is a companion book to *Olivia's Opposites*, introduced in the section "First Words." In *Olivia Counts*, youngsters can learn the counting numbers 1 through 10, while viewing the appealing piglet Olivia with various numbered objects. It begins with one ball and ends with Olivia pictured in 10 various familiar poses, such as trying on pantyhose, standing on her head, wearing flippers, listening to headphones, jumping rope, sunbathing, and doing handstands. My favorite page is *four aunts*, all of whom look like an older Olivia.

***See and Spy Counting* by Julie Aigner-Clark, illustrated by Nadeem Zaidi. (2001). Baby Einstein. 16 pages.** Toddlers can sharpen their visual acuity while learning the numerals and counting numbers 1 through 5 by spotting objects and then counting how many of those items appear in the picture. Double-page spreads feature different animals in appropriate settings, such as a cow on a farm. Each spread contains five questions, and children are encouraged to see and count, for example, the number of barns (1) and the number of ears on the cow (2). For each page, the answers are always in numerical order, 1 through 5, making this an excellent first counting book.

Shapes

Similar to the counting numbers and colors, basic geometric shapes are concepts that children are required to demonstrate before they are ready to leave kindergarten. If children can learn them before they enter kindergarten, they are at a great advantage. The following books will help them acquire these concepts.

See and Spy Shapes by Julie Aigner-Clark, illustrated by Nadeem Zaidi. (2001). Baby Einstein. 16 pages. Youngsters will love looking at the simple but brightly colored illustrations and listening to the rhyming text in this book. Start by pointing out each shape and saying its name: circle, square, triangle, rectangle, oval, star, and diamond. (Later, you can reinforce these concepts by pointing out the shapes of familiar objects at home, during play, or while riding in the car.) After children become familiar with the distinctive characteristics of the basic shapes, they will enjoy independently spotting them in the book's illustrations and then counting how many of each shape they can find. Each page features a different poem, animal, and shape, so numbers, colors, and animals are reinforced along with the basic shapes.

Puzzling Shapes: A Puzzle Book by Julie Aigner-Clark, illustrated by Nadeem Zaidi. (2002). Baby Einstein. 12 pages. This unique book is both a shape concept book and an interaction book (discussed in the last section of this chapter). Removable puzzle pieces made from colorful, heavy cardboard will both entertain children and help them develop their eye–hand coordination. Children can take out the puzzle pieces one at a time, while you discuss the shape, relative size, and color of each. After a few experiences with the book, children may enjoy taking out several pieces at one time and then determining where they belong in the book. On the last pages, the shapes are all the same color, so children can practice identifying them without the aid of color cues. However, the pieces are small enough for young children to put inside their mouths, so they should only view this book with supervision. In addition, the pieces are not easy to snap into place, so little ones may need your help to make them fit.

Other Concepts

Some books for infants and toddlers are primarily entertaining, but they also serve as a stimulus for discussion of interesting concepts, such as seasons of the year, daily activities, and community helpers. While they do not have full plots, these books do contain characters, setting, and events.

I Am a Bunny by Ole Risom, illustrated by Richard Scarry. (1963). Golden Books. 26 pages. Nicholas, dressed in adorable red overalls and a yellow shirt, is a bunny who lives in a hollow tree and enjoys all the seasons of the year. In the spring, Nicholas likes to pick flowers and chase butterflies (who chase him back). In the summer, Nicholas lies in the sun and watches birds in the sky and frogs in the pond. In the fall, Nicholas enjoys watching the leaves fall and observing the animals prepare for winter. When winter arrives, Nicholas sees snow falling, and then he curls up snug in his bunny bed in the hollow tree to dream about the coming spring.

Olivia by Ian Falconer. (2000). Atheneum. 40 pages. In the first of Falconer's books about Olivia, an irresistible piglet of boundless energy, children learn about a typical play day. However, the energetic Olivia is very talented; her sandcastle resembles a Manhattan skyscraper, and her wall scribbling resembles museum art. Olivia is also good at singing 40 very loud songs, and she is very good at wearing people out (including herself). In this day in the life of Olivia, we learn she likes the beach, dressing up, and dancing, but not taking naps. She envisions herself as a prima ballerina, and she is not beyond negotiating the number of books for her mother to read at bedtime. Falconer's spare text spotlights the illustrations that serve as visual punch lines. These highly amusing illustrations are charcoal portraits against a white background that are spotted with bright reds for the clothing or objects used by Olivia.

The Fire Engine Book by Diane Muldrow, illustrated by Tibor Gergely. (1950). Golden Books. 24 pages. In this action-filled book, children can experience the exciting ride of old firefighting vehicles—the fire chief's car, the hose truck, and the hook-and-ladder truck with several firefighters hanging on alongside and one steering in the back. All the while the bells ring "clang, clang." When the firefighters arrive at the antique store, they hook up the hoses to the fire hydrant, use their axes to get in, and rescue precious store items (including a puppy by jumping with it into the net), while giving the flames a good dousing. As one might expect for a book first published in 1950, the heroes are all males, but the old fire trucks with the pet Dalmatian riding in front make for a thrilling reading experience.

Once Upon a Potty by Alona Frankel. (1979). HarperFestival. 48 pages. Potty training can be a long and stressful process for some parents and children. A book that explains it on a child's level may make the transition from diapers to toilet a little easier. *Once Upon a Potty* comes in two versions: The boy version has a character named Joshua, and the girl version features Prudence. Both books open with a very round (and nude) child who shows his or her body parts, such as eyes for seeing and legs for walking. The child also explains he or she has a *pee-pee* for making *wee-wee* and a bottom for sitting (with a little hole for making *poo-poo*). Some readers may find the illustrations with the children bending over to show the hole in their bottoms to be overly gross, but the book does a good job of explaining the process of why and how children use a potty. However, many parents prefer that their children learn the anatomical names of their body parts rather than the baby talk used in this book. In addition, children today use potty chairs, but the book's potty is an 18th-century chamber pot, looking more like an oversized coffee mug! Nonetheless, the humor and cute illustrations will get children interested in the book and possibly the process of potty training as well.

Because that little hole in one's bottom does not actually *make* the poo-poo, you may wish to also share *Everyone Poops* by Taro Gomi, which charmingly explains the process of eating and eliminating waste through its humorous text and illustrations of both people (father and boy) and multiple animals—all of whom poop, of course.

Devotional

Several best-selling books were specially written for Christian parents to share with children who are ready for something more than bible stories. Best-selling books about other religions—even on the weekly lists—are rare. Therefore, I have included books about other religions in chapter 7, "Selecting Books to Supplement the Bestsellers." Moreover, a search on Amazon.com or another large Internet bookstore can help you find additional books about your religion to share. This can be especially important for many parents because children are not likely to encounter these books in public schools, and yet knowledge of religions is important to understand the multicultural world in which we live.

Poems and Prayers for the Very Young selected and illustrated by Martha Alexander. (1973). Random House. 32 pages.** This short collection contains 39 poems with spiritual and inspirational themes—all understandable by young children. A number are classic poems by well-known poets, such as Ralph Waldo Emerson's "Father, We Thank Thee," Robert Browning's "Song," Christina Rossetti's "Who Has Seen the Wind," Robert Louis Stevenson's "Rain," Jane Taylor's "Twinkle, Twinkle, Little Star," and William Blake's "Night." The collection also includes a few traditional poems with unknown authors, such as "Bedtime Prayer": "Now I lay me down to sleep, I pray Thee Lord, Thy child to keep. Thy love guard me through the night, and wake me with the morning light." The anthologist also illustrated the book with simple but colorful pictures of young children in their daily activities.

Blessings Every Day: 365 Simple Devotions for the Very Young by Carla Barnhill, illustrated by Elena Kucharik. (2001). Tyndale. 384 pages. This collection of devotions is a broad introduction to the bible and its many promises. The book features a scripture for each day of the year, followed by cheerful text that connects the verses with young children's experiences and daily issues. A short poem or prayer and colorful illustrations enhance each page. Though many parents use the daily reading as a bedtime devotional, I suggest sharing it right after children finish breakfast so they may ponder and apply the teaching throughout their day.

God Made You Special by Eric Metaxas. (2002). ZonderKidz. 18 pages. Through rhymes, humor, and lovable veggies, little ones hear about how God makes everyone special. The characters explain that God made each of us different and unique, and he loves us very much. Bob the tomato is red and round, and he bounces because he has no feet; Madame Blueberry lives in a tree, and she is special because she is blue. The French Peas are special because they speak with a French accent. This book will help children understand that it is okay to be different and that being different makes them special. Other popular books by Eric Metaxas include *Even Fish Slappers Need a Second Chance* and *Jonah and the Pirates Who Usually Don't Do Anything*.

Secrets of the Vine for Little Ones by Bruce H. Wilkinson and Melody Carlson, illustrated by Alexi Natchev. (2002). Tommy Nelson. 14 pages. In a gentle poem, Melody Carlson has distilled the essence of Bruce H. Wilkinson's best-selling adult book *Secrets of the Vine*, making it appropriate for young children. In this book, they will hear how God cares for them with tenderness and love. The content is based on Jesus's teachings that God is the vinedresser (caretaker); He is the vine, and Christians are His branches. Parents may wish to use this book during devotional time to help children understand the application of Jesus's teachings about "bearing fruit" in their lives.

Prayers for Children **by Eloise Wilkin. (1952). Golden Books. 24 pages.** This book is a short collection of traditional prayers, most with unknown authors. Eloise Wilkin, who did the artwork for many of the early Little Golden Books, touchingly illustrated it. Though some of the vocabulary may be difficult for very young children, the lilting language is sure to please them, and the reverent language will convey the essence of each prayer.

The Prayer of Jabez for Little Ones **by Bruce H. Wilkinson and Melody Carlson, illustrated by Alexi Natchev. (2001). Tommy Nelson. 14 pages.** The text of this little board book is a child's prayer, based on the well-known prayer of Jabez in I Chronicles 4:10 of the bible. The purpose of this book is to help children learn to pray and to understand that a loving and strong God listens and keeps them safe. The prayer asks that God would bless them, enlarge their territory (aspirations), protect them, and keep them from evil. It concludes with four questions for parents and children to discuss.

Interaction

Interaction books—also called participation books—are especially made for busy hands and curious minds. They contain lift-up flaps to look under for hidden objects, textured pages to feel, parts that move, scented pages, and sometimes a center pop-up as well. I have saved them for last in this chapter because most of these books would not last long in the hands of children under 2 years of age (especially the nicely scented pages, which might be tempting to teething youngsters). In addition, some of the detachable pieces could present a choking hazard. Interaction books are great for lap reading, but I suggest you set them out of sight when you are not around to guide younger children through the moveable parts on each page.

Pat the Bunny **by Dorothy Kunhardt. (1940). Golden Books. 18 pages.** The all-time best-selling interaction book is *Pat the Bunny*. Dorothy Kunhardt's interactive book for toddlers was the first of its kind when it was originally published in 1940. Children can participate with the characters Paul and Judy in seven activities. They can pat the bunny's (fake) fur, lift a small cloth to play peek-a-boo with Paul, smell the scented flower illustration, see a reflection in the shiny film, feel the sandpaper representing Daddy's scratchy face, and even look at a tiny seven-page bunny book within this book. Last, children are invited to poke their finger in the hole that represents Mummy's wedding ring. At the end, they are asked to wave bye-bye. Simple line drawings and pastel colors make this an easy book for even infants to focus on, and the double-folded cardboard pages (inside which the textured objects are attached) will withhold repeated use. This book is available in hardcover, paperback, and spiral-bound (plastic comb).

Parents who may have grown weary of reading *Pat the Bunny* to their children "just one more time, please" will get many laughs from the parody of it (for adults and intermediate-grade children), titled *Pat the Beastie: A Pull-and-Poke Book* by Henrik Drescher. In this book, two children play pranks on their patient pet Beastie (a green-haired, dragon-type critter), and they offer readers the chance to do the same. All the while, a toothy bird and dog utter warnings and reproaches to the children for more humane treatment of Beastie (who ends the abuse by gulping them down at the end)—a bit gross, but certainly comic relief for adults.

***Where's Spot?* by Eric Hill. (1980). Putnam. 22 pages.** Spot is a puppy who does not want to eat his dinner, so he hides in a basket. His mother searches throughout the house, and she finds eight other animals that are hiding there before finding Spot. Children participate in the search for Spot by lifting up flaps to reveal the concealed animals.

***Fuzzy Yellow Ducklings* by Matthew Van Fleet. (1995). Dial Books for Young Readers. 16 pages.** This book is unique because not only is it an interactive book but it is also a multiple concept book, demonstrating numbers, textures, colors, shapes, and animals. Fuzzy yellow ducklings, bumpy brown frogs, fuzzy gray koalas, woolly white sheep, and other types of creatures are concealed behind die-cut panels in which viewers are presented only with a labeled (and textured) shape, such as a circle, crescent, oval, or line. When you turn the page, the rest of the creature's body is revealed along with his friends (increasing by one for each shape). My favorite is a sticky pink line that turns out to be a frog's tongue tangled with eight others during their efforts to catch flies.

The Wheels on the Bus by Paul O. Zelinsky. (1990). Dutton. 16 pages. Few children have never heard the traditional song "The Wheels on the Bus." Paul O. Zelinsky masterfully illustrated this old song in an interactive book with moving parts: The wheels turn 'round and 'round, doors open and shut, and tabs pull wipers back and forth (swish, swish, swish). After a few readings, and with a little encouragement, children can pick out several subplots within the details of the illustrations—a boy with a boxful of adventurous kittens, a motorcyclist and her runaway puppy, and a young man with a guitar. The bus's last stop is the library, where a folk singer is singing (you guessed it) "The Wheels on the Bus." The back cover contains the musical notation to sing or play along.

Open the Barn Door, Find a Cow by Christopher Santoro. (1993). Random House. 22 pages. In this colorful lift-the-flap book, youngsters find out what is in a barn, under a hen, in a sty, and more. They can literally open the barn door and take a tour around the barnyard to find out which animal makes the sounds in the text. After several readings, children may want to knock on the door before opening it, and then mimic the animated animal noises of the character underneath. (I especially like the goat who is chewing on a sock.)

No Biting! by Karen Katz. (2002). Grosset & Dunlap. 14 pages. In this funny lift-the-flap book, the frustrated toddlers decide to hit and bite—playmates, Mommy, and even the family pet. However, when viewers lift the flaps, they will discover that the toddlers know a better way to act, and it is better to say "no" to hitting, biting, pushing, kicking, and spitting, and to say "yes" to fun things like playing a drum when they feel like hitting something.

My First Jumbo Book of Colors by James Diaz and Melanie Gerth. (2002). Cartwheel Books. 10 pages. This color concept book is full of interactive parts that are designed to keep little fingers busy. In the brightly colored pictures, children can pull the blue train along the track, touch the soft yellow chick, and move the red crab through the water. Once children are introduced to the three primary colors, they can use wheels and flaps to pretend to mix paint and create new colors.

Tails by Matthew Van Fleet. (2003). Red Wagon. 20 pages. With rhymed text, textured illustrations, lift-up flaps, fold-out pages, and scratch-and-sniff spots, youngsters can learn animal names, shapes, colors, numbers, and—best of all—textures. A menagerie of playful animals sport all types of tails, such as bumpy (alligator), fuzzy (tiger), stinky (scratch-and-sniff skunk)—not to mention furry, spiny, and shiny tails. Pull-tabs will even make some of the tails swish or wag.

Book cover from *Tootle* by Gertrude Crampton, illustrated by Tibor Gergely. © 1945, renewed 1973 by Random House, Inc. Used by permission of Golden Books, an imprint of Random House Children's Books, a division of Random House, Inc.

Chapter 4

Best–Selling Books for Children Ages 3–4

In the position statement *Literacy Development in the Preschool Years* (2005), the International Reading Association affirms, "The preschool years, ages 3 and 4, are extremely important for children's social, emotional, physical, cognitive, and language and literacy development. Children's development can be affected by high-quality preschool experiences that can improve later academic and social competence" (p. 2). The experiences that foster early language and literacy development include story reading, dramatic play, storytelling, and retelling stories. In this chapter, you will read about books that lend themselves especially well to these critical experiences.

By the time children are 3 years old, they are able to view hardcover picture books independently. I recommend you tell them that books are not like toys and that they need special care to last a long time. (This is important when progressing from board books to books with regular paper pages.) Young children may occasionally need gentle reminders to turn the pages slowly and, when they are finished, to put their books back on the shelf (rather than in a toy box or left on the floor). When you see that children are properly caring for their hardcover books, you can give them the less sturdy, and less costly, paperback books.

Unlike the concept books for children ages 1–2, the books targeted for 3- and 4-year-olds are primarily picture storybooks—most with full plots containing characters, setting, problem, goal, events, and a resolution.

Animal Fantasy

In animal fantasy stories, the main characters are always animals that possess human speech and can think and express emotions like humans. Often the characters live entirely like humans, wearing clothing, residing in houses, and cooking food. Because of the popularity of animal fantasy, it is not surprising that animal fantasy makes up the largest section of this chapter.

Little Golden Book Treasury

Five books in Golden's classic library, called the Little Golden Book Treasury, have reached bestseller status, and three are animal fantasies. Most of these books were first published nearly six decades ago, so, like me, you may have owned them as a child. My mother bought them in the grocery store for a quarter. The books are still popular with children today because their stories are timeless (but they do cost more than a quarter now).

The Poky Little Puppy by Janette Sebring Lowrey, illustrated by Gustaf Tenggren. (1942). Golden Books. 24 pages. *The Poky Little Puppy* is the all-time best-selling children's picture book according to *Publishers Weekly*. Nearly 15 million copies of Lowrey's book have sold in the United States alone during the first 58 years since its original publication. This cumulative tale is about five puppies that mischievously dig under the fence to explore the outside world. When they smell dinner, all but the poky puppy run home. They are scolded by their mother, and then they go to bed without dessert. After his mother is asleep, the poky puppy returns home through the hole under the fence and eats up everyone's dessert. This continues for three days, but on the third night, the brothers and sisters fill the hole, and their mother gives them all the dessert.

The Saggy Baggy Elephant by Kathryn Jackson and Byron Jackson, illustrated by Gustaf Tenggren. (1947). Golden Books. 24 pages. Sooki is a baby elephant who loves to dance even though it makes the jungle shake. He has never seen other animals like himself, so when the parrot tells him his skin is all saggy and baggy, he tries to make himself look better by exercising and then soaking in water (hoping his skin will shrink). Other animals in the jungle are more interested in how Sooki tastes instead of how he looks, so after escaping a tiger and a crocodile, he hides in a cave. Unfortunately, the cave belongs to a hungry lion. When Sooki's frightened trumpeting brings forth a herd of animals just like him, he is rescued from the lion. The other elephants assure Sooki that he is a perfectly dandy little elephant, not an ugly saggy baggy animal, and together they dance away in the jungle.

Tawny Scrawny Lion by Kathryn Jackson, illustrated by Gustaf Tenggren. (1952). Golden Books. 24 pages. The tawny scrawny lion is always hungry. He has to run so hard to chase down the other animals that no matter how many he eats, his ribs are always showing and he is still hungry. When the monkeys, kangaroos, zebras, bears, camels, and elephants see a fat little rabbit hopping through the forest picking berries, they appoint him their spokesperson. The naive rabbit invites the lion home to have supper with his nine sisters and brothers, and the lion greedily accepts. However, the rabbit stops along the way to gather more berries as well as mushrooms, herbs, and a few fresh fish for their nightly carrot stew. After the lion eats his fill of the delicious stew, he is too full to eat the little rabbits. Later, he decides to contribute ingredients for the rabbits' daily meal instead of eating the other animals.

The "If You Give..." Series

Laura Joffe Numeroff's series contains great examples of pattern books, which do not tell stories, but rather take the reader through a series of similar incidents in which only one thing changes. In this case, a child gives an animal something to eat and sets off a chain reaction of requests, in which each item fetched results in an additional need (prime examples of "If you give them an inch, they'll take a mile"). For this and other series, I am including only the three top-selling books, although many more books in the series may have achieved bestseller status.

If You Give a Mouse a Cookie by Laura Joffe Numeroff, illustrated by Felicia Bond. (1985). Laura Geringer. 32 pages. When a boy offers a tiny mouse a cookie, he does not suspect that the bossy little creature will wear him out. For example, the mouse certainly needs a glass of milk to wash down that cookie, and you cannot expect him to drink the milk without a straw, can you? By the time the boy is finished granting all the mouse's urgent requests—and cleaning up after him—the boy is exhausted. The narrator's warped logic not only provides giggles but also an opportunity for discussion of cause and effect.

If You Give a Moose a Muffin by Laura Joffe Numeroff, illustrated by Felicia Bond. (1991). Laura Geringer. 32 pages. If a big, hungry moose comes to visit, you might give him a muffin to make him feel at home, but if you give him a muffin, he will want some jam to go with it. The young host is again run ragged by a surprise guest who—once he has finished off all the muffins—

wants to make more, which entails a trip to the store. The action of the book principally involves putting on a puppet show, from the creation of sock puppets and scenery through cleanup. Although the mother is absent from the first book, she appears in several illustrations (but not the text) in this sequel, yet she seems to be oblivious to all that is going on.

***If You Give a Pig a Pancake* by Laura Joffe Numeroff, illustrated by Felicia Bond. (1998). Laura Geringer. 32 pages.** When the aroma of pancakes attracts a piglet to the window of a little girl who is cooking breakfast, it sets off a chain reaction. The accommodating little girl tries to keep up with the whims of the little pig after offering her a pancake. Of course, the piglet is sure to want some maple syrup to go with it. And when she eats that, she gets sticky and needs to take a bath (where she asks for bubbles and a toy). The funny formula creates anticipation in the listener, and the illustrations provide plenty of visual humor. Some doting parents may see themselves in the girl's struggles to meet the pig's increasingly elaborate demands.

The Little Critter Series

Mercer Mayer's series of books about Little Critter (who looks a bit like a toothy beaver without a tail) has made him one of the most popular author–illustrators of books for young children. Funny incidents in the warm relationships between the endearing Little Critter and his family are the hallmarks of this series. With minimal text, Little Critter narrates the books from a child's point of view, but the real episodes are told through the illustrations from an adult's point of view. Because of this, Mayer's books are excellent for children's development of visual literacy, the ability to obtain meaning from graphic stimuli. Long before children are able to read, they can learn to obtain ideas and meaning from pictures. During book sharing, help children focus on the elements of each illustration that go beyond the written text in telling the story, and encourage them to describe what they see (see Richards & Anderson, 2003). Then, even after children learn to read, illustrations can continue to aid their comprehension.

***Just Me and My Dad* by Mercer Mayer. (1975). Golden Books. 24 pages.** A father-and-son camping trip is filled with Little Critter's good intentions (and mishaps), but in spite of difficulties, they pitch their tent, catch fish for dinner, and sleep beneath the stars. Camping alone with Dad is an exciting adventure, and Father lets Little Critter participate in as many ways as possible, despite his foul-ups, such as launching the canoe too hard and making it sink. The book ends with them sleeping in their tent all night long, making this a perfect book for child and father bonding. A small grasshopper and a spider humorously accompany the father and Little Critter in every scene, and children are sure to point them out. After a couple of readings, encourage children to tell the story from the grasshopper and spider's point of view.

Just Go to Bed by Mercer Mayer. (1985). Golden Books. 24 pages. In perhaps his most precious book, Mercer Mayer illustrates how the energetic and imaginative Little Critter resists his father's efforts to get him ready for bed by pretending he is a cowboy, army general, space cadet, sea monster, zookeeper, and a horde of other characters. The equally imaginative father plays along and thinks of ways to move the child (in his various role-plays) through bath time, snack time, pajama time, and (after the father loses patience) sleep time.

Just Grandma and Me by Mercer Mayer. (1975). Golden Books. 24 pages. A trip to the beach with Grandma provides lots of fun, such as snorkeling, swimming, and building sand castles. Little Critter is a good helper, and he means well, but things do not always turn out right. For example, when Grandma's hot dog falls in the sand, he washes it off (in the salty ocean), and though he says he will blow up the inflatable seahorse, he needs a little help in the end. Once again, the grasshopper and spider accompany Little Critter in every scene. Because the text never mentions them, they provide a great opportunity for children to retell the story from another viewpoint. Mayer has many more bestsellers in the Little Critter series, notably *Merry Christmas, Mom and Dad*; *Just for You*; and *All by Myself*.

The Rainbow Fish Series

The unique beauty of Marcus Pfister's Rainbow Fish series is achieved through silver foil stamping that glitters on every page, complementing the gorgeous illustrations in pleasing shades of lavender and blue. *The Rainbow Fish* was first published in Switzerland, and it became an international bestseller. The other books in the series never achieved bestseller status, but they are still great books to read. They include *Rainbow Fish to the Rescue*, *Rainbow Fish and the Sea Monsters' Cave*, and *Rainbow Fish and the Big Blue Whale*.

The Rainbow Fish **by Marcus Pfister, translated by J. Alison James. (1992). North–South Books. 26 pages.** The Rainbow Fish is the most beautiful in the entire ocean with scales of every shade of blue, green, purple, and sparkling silver. However, he is proud and silent, and he ignores the calls of his admirers to come and play. After he rudely scoffs at a little blue fish who asks for one of his scales, the other fish shun him. His dazzling, shimmering scales bring him no happiness when no one admires them, so he takes the advice of the wise octopus who tells him that to be happy he must give a glittering scale to each of the other fish. After giving away all but one of his silver scales, he discovers the real value of personal beauty and friendship.

The Little Animal Series

Judy Dunn uses adorable photographs to illustrate how small farm animals live and mature. Dunn conveys much interesting information about the various species in her brief storylines.

The Little Duck **by Judy Dunn, illustrated by Phoebe Dunn. (1976). Random House. 32 pages.** In Dunn's most popular book, attractive full-color photographs and a simple story provide a realistic, but humorous, account of the first year of life of Henry, a little duckling whose egg is discovered near a pond by the (nameless) boy who is fishing there. The boy takes the egg home and uses an incubator to hatch it. As Henry grows, the boy makes a number of mistakes, which you would not want children to model, such as putting the hatchling into a wading pond before it can swim and then using a hairdryer to dry it off (not to mention bringing home a wild egg in the first place). Henry loves to follow the boy around the farm and to sit in Grandpa's lap while he reads the newspaper. However, Henry gets lonely after the boy goes back to school, so he wanders off to the same pond where he was found (as an egg), and he meets a female duck who joins him to start their own family.

The Little Rabbit **by Judy Dunn, illustrated by Phoebe Dunn. (1980). Random House. 32 pages.** In full-color photographs, the cuddly world of a real rabbit family is introduced to young readers. Sarah receives a little rabbit in her Easter basket and names her Buttercup. She lovingly feeds and cares for Buttercup each day, and they become constant companions. When Sarah falls asleep in the meadow near their home, Buttercup wanders off and gets into trouble. While this might be the end of a little rabbit in real life, no serious consequences arise in this story. Eventually Buttercup gives birth to seven little bunnies, which Sarah names after the days of the week, and when they are old enough to leave their mother, she gives them away to friends.

***The Little Lamb* by Judy Dunn, illustrated by Phoebe Dunn. (1977). Random House. 32 pages.** Colorful photographs illuminate this appealing story of Emmy, a young girl who takes care of a newborn lamb over the course of a summer. She names him Timothy and cares for him much like a mother would her baby by feeding him milk from a bottle, lavishing him with affection, and joyfully playing with him each day. The lamb has a number of misadventures, such as knocking over a bucket of apples. However, when Timothy accidentally pulls down a picnic table full of food at a birthday party, Emmy's father says that he is too big to keep as a pet and must rejoin his flock at the adjacent Wetherbee farm. Emmy gives up her beloved pet but knows he is close enough to visit regularly.

Other Animal Fantasy Books

Following are some great animal fantasy books that are not part of a series.

***It's Not Easy Being a Bunny* by Marilyn Sadler, illustrated by Roger Bollen. (1983). Random House. 48 pages.** P.J. Funnybunny is very sad because he does not like being a bunny. He has to eat cooked carrots every day, his house is crowded with far too many brothers and sisters, and he does not like having such big ears. So, he takes off, deciding to become a bear. When hibernation gets dull, he tries being a bird. And so it continues, with beavers, pigs, opossums, moose, and skunks (all of whom warmly welcome P.J.). Finally, P.J. realizes that being a bunny is not so bad. The short, repetitive text and bright, humorous cartoons keep young children's attention while providing lots of giggles. In the first reading, encourage children to use higher order thinking skills by predicting what problem P.J. is going to encounter living with the next group of animals.

***Frederick* by Leo Lionni. (1967). Knopf. 32 pages.** Frederick lives with four other field mice in the old stone wall in the meadow, which is close to the abandoned farmhouse and empty granary. While the other mice are gathering food for the winter, Frederick seems to daydream the summer away. He tells them only that he is gathering sunrays, colors, and words. When the dreary and bitter-cold winter comes, and the food is nearly gone, Frederick warms the hearts and cheers the spirits of his companions with his descriptions of the golden glow of sunlight, the beautiful colors of the meadow, and the glory of the passing seasons in beautiful poetic words. In this way, the long and cold days of winter pass more quickly. I also recommend Lionni's *Swimmy*.

Biscuit by Alyssa Satin Capucilli, illustrated by Pat Schories. (1996). HarperTrophy. 32 pages. Biscuit is a little yellow puppy who (repeatedly) wants just one more thing before he will go to sleep (much like the children who read the book): snack, drink, hug and kiss, story, blanket and doll, and covers tucked in. However, he is still not satisfied, and in the end, he gets what he really wants—to sleep next to the little girl.

Angelina Ballerina by Katharine Holabird, illustrated by Helen Craig. (2002). American Girl. 24 pages. Angelina is a wee, white mouseling who loves to dance to the exclusion of all other activities. She will not clean her room, help clear the table, or listen to her parents because she is dancing every waking moment. Everything changes when her parents decide to take her interest seriously. Mr. and Mrs. Mouseling go shopping, and they return with a lovely ballerina's tutu. Angelina starts ballet lessons, and then she does the chores her parents want because she can dance all she wants in class and recitals.

Daisy Comes Home by Jan Brett. (2002). Putnam. 32 pages. Jan Brett is best known for her engaging artwork, including intricate border designs that advance the plots of her books, often by depicting scenes that are not revealed in the text. In *Daisy Comes Home*, readers learn of Daisy, an unhappy hen in China who is the smallest of Mei Mei's flock of six. The larger hens constantly pick on her and push her off the perch. At the end of a rainy day, she escapes from the henhouse and sleeps in an egg basket by the river's edge, unaware of the rising water. When she awakens, she is floating down the Li River past picturesque villages, animal-shaped mountains, and dangerous river animals. She escapes a barking dog, a snorting water buffalo, and some curious monkeys. However, a greedy fisherman catches her and takes her to the market. Mei Mei searches frantically for Daisy but eventually has to go to the market to sell the eggs she collected. There, a friend warns her that someone has her egg basket with Daisy. She calls Daisy at the top of her voice, and together they escape. Bret frames her stunning illustrations, which depict the Guang Xi Province of China, with designs of bamboo poles that are embellished with basket weaves, painted pottery, and story characters.

How Do Dinosaurs Say Goodnight? **by Jane Yolen, illustrated by Mark Teague. (2000). Blue Sky Press. 40 pages.** In playful verse and humorous pictures, a mother and child ponder the different ways a dinosaur can say goodnight. Substituting dinosaurs for children makes the various postponement antics hilarious, from yawning and fussing to throwing toys. Illustrations show a variety of human mothers and fathers trying to put their dinosaur children to bed, including Tyrannosaurus Rex, Triceratops, Stegosaurus, and seven others—all with names incorporated somewhere into their pictures, such as with alphabet blocks on the bedroom floor.

How Do Dinosaurs Get Well Soon? **by Jane Yolen, illustrated by Mark Teague. (2003). Blue Sky Press. 40 pages.** Yolen addresses children's fears about being sick by posing the question, "What if a dinosaur catches the flu?" The negative behaviors these dinosaurs demonstrate, including whimpering, whining, littering with dirty tissues, flinging medicine, and tossing covers are all frowned upon. These negative behaviors are intensified at the doctor's office by dragging feet, clamping mouths, screaming, and hiding. What dinosaurs are supposed to do is drink lots of juice, rest, use a hankie, and take medicine. As each ailing creature is introduced, look for the name of the species hidden somewhere within the double-page spread.

Merry Christmas, Big Hungry Bear! **by Audrey Wood, illustrated by Don Wood. (2002). Blue Sky Press. 48 pages.** Little Mouse beams at all the presents piled high under his Christmas tree; however, he hears about Big Hungry Bear who lives in a cold, dark cave at the top of the hill, who loves Christmas, but never gets any presents—not even from Santa. At first Little Mouse tries to protect his heap of gifts by anxiously setting up padlocks and barricades and fearfully guarding them. Then he begins to feel sorry for the bear. He gathers together most of his gifts, puts on his Santa suit, and bravely makes his way to Bear's den, where he delivers the gifts and decorates a Christmas tree. The mysterious Big Hungry Bear (never actually appearing in the pictures) is not so scary after all, and readers are left thinking that perhaps a new friendship between a tiny mouse and a big bear is possible.

Kitten's First Full Moon **by Kevin Henkes. (2004). Greenwillow Books. 40 pages.** A young kitten sees the full moon for the first time, and she thinks it is a bowl of milk in the sky. She tries to lick the faraway moon and gets a bug on her tongue. Next, she launches herself into the air, paws reaching out for the bowl, but she only tumbles down the stairs. Then she chases the moon through the garden and field to the pond, where she climbs a tree. She is surprised to see a bigger milk bowl shining in the water and dives in after it. No matter how hard she tries, there is still that elusive little bowl of milk that is so tempting. Her persistence finally gives out, and she returns home to find that, miraculously, a real little bowl of milk is waiting for her at home. Kevin Henkes used charcoal and a cream-colored palette to form thick black lines and shades of grey to depict the luminous moonlit night.

Animated Object Fantasy

Many young children fantasize that their toys, especially dolls and stuffed animals, are alive. You will often hear them talking to their toys and then talking for their toys as they answer back. Can you imagine what it would be like if toys and other inanimate objects really could speak and move about? Authors of animated object fantasy stories bring to life inanimate objects such as stuffed animals, railroad engines, and plants.

Tootle **by Gertrude Crampton, illustrated by Tibor Gergely. (1945). Golden Books. 24 pages.** The baby locomotives all go to school in Lower Trainswitch to learn to be big locomotives. Bill, the old engineer, is head of the school, and he teaches them that the most important lessons are to stay on the rails no matter what happens and to stop for a waving red flag. Bill's favorite student is little Tootle, whom he envisions will grow up to be a two-miles-a-minute Flyer between New York and Chicago. However, one day, Tootle decides to jump off the tracks to race a swift black horse through the meadow. For several days after the race, Tootle plays in the meadow, chasing butterflies among the buttercups, daisies, and hollyhocks. Bill thinks of a plan to get Tootle to stay on the tracks by having all the townspeople hide in the meadow and wave a red flag whenever Tootle comes near. In the end, Tootle gets back on the tracks, conforms to his training, and grows up to be a big Flyer. (Adult readers may experience sadness knowing the carefree, joyful playtime in the meadow was lost forever to the world of work and responsibilities.)

Thomas the Tank Engine **by Wilbert Awdry. (1946). Random House. 32 pages.** The Reverend Wilbert Awdry launched the Railway Series with *Thomas the Tank Engine* in 1946. Like the main character in *Tootle*, Thomas is a train, but instead of running on steam made from burning coal, he carries his own fuel oil in a tank. Thomas has six small wheels and a short, stumpy funnel, boiler, and dome. He lives at a big station and pulls coaches to the big engines who take them on long journeys. This sassy little engine often grumbles that none of the other engines works as hard as he does. This makes him cross, impatient, and even rude to the other engines. One day, Gordon the big engine decides to teach him a lesson and takes off with Thomas coupled to his rear. After a terrifying ride, being pulled faster than he could ever travel by himself, Thomas realizes he is not as strong as he thought. After another terrifying ride in which freight cars push Thomas down the hill, he learns he is not as clever as he thought. However, after proving himself to be a "Really Useful Engine" by running the breakdown train so workers could repair the line and get the new engine, James, back on the line, he is given a branch line all to himself with two coaches.

Thomas Gets Tricked by Wilbert Awdry. (1989). Random House. 24 pages. Like the other Thomas volumes, there are four short stories in this book. In the title story, Thomas blows off steam, literally, by teasing the proudest and biggest engine of all, but he learns to think twice after he pulls his first big passenger train. "Come Out, Henry!" "Henry to the Rescue," and "A Big Day for Thomas" are the other stories. Illustrations are full-color photographs of dioramas, giving a three-dimensional effect.

Catch Me, Catch Me! by Wilbert Awdry, illustrated by Owain Bell. (1990). Random House. 24 pages. Thomas wants to race the mighty—and pompous—Gordon, who is bigger, stronger, and faster than he is, because Thomas believes it takes more than size, strength, and speed to win a race. Therefore, they set off to see who can get to the other side of the hill first. Thomas falls behind, but he finds a shortcut through a tunnel, too small for the larger train, and he ends up in front, showing that quick thinking can also help one succeed. Included is a page of word cards to cut out (one for each of the 50 different words in the story) with descriptions of six games to play with the cards to help children practice concentration, word recognition, matching, and rhyming as well as making sentences.

Scuffy the Tugboat by Gertrude Crampton, illustrated by Tibor Gergely. (1946). Golden Books. 24 pages. Scuffy is a little toy tugboat who is painted red with a blue smokestack. He is cross because he knows he was meant for bigger things than sitting on a toy store shelf, so the owner takes Scuffy home to his little boy, who tries to sail him in the bathtub. However, Scuffy is still cross because he knows he was meant for bigger things than floating in a bathtub, so the boy and his father take him to a brook. Scuffy enjoys the fast brook so much that he allows it to carry him downstream away from the boy and man who chase after him. Scuffy enjoys the sights and excitement of his first day, but when night falls, he becomes frightened. The next day, the brook joins another to form a small river, and as Scuffy sails along, the water becomes wider, deeper, and scarier. When the melted snow makes the river flood, Scuffy encounters danger as he rushes past villages, sawmills, and bridges. Finally, he passes through a large city where the river meets the sea, and he sees that there is no end to the massive body of water ahead. There he longs to be back safely with the boy and his father, who just happen to be standing on a pier and grab him before he is lost at sea.

Corduroy by Don Freeman. (1968). Viking Press. 32 pages. Corduroy is a stuffed bear who is dressed in green corduroy overalls. He lives on a shelf in the toy area of a big department store, waiting for someone to come along and take him home. When Lisa, a young African American girl, sees him, she knows immediately that he is what she has been looking for, but her mother says he does not look new because he has lost the button to a shoulder strap. After the store has closed for the evening, Corduroy goes exploring in search of his lost button. He gets lost in the furniture department, but the security guard finds him hiding under the covers of a big bed and takes him back to the toy shelf. The next morning, after Lisa has taken money from her piggy bank, she goes to the store to buy Corduroy. After taking him home, she sews a new button onto his overalls. Lisa and Corduroy are secure, knowing they have each found a friend.

Love

Love continues to be a theme in books for 3- and 4-year-olds as it is in books for younger children. It is important to reassure children that you love them unconditionally, and the books that follow are a beautiful way to convey this.

Love You Forever by Robert N. Munsch, illustrated by Sheila McGraw. (1986). Firefly. 32 pages. At the beginning of the book, a young woman holds her newborn son. She lovingly rocks him to sleep while singing her own lullaby that assures him she will love him forever and that he will be her baby as long as she is living. Subsequent pages show snippets of the boy's life as a 2-year-old, a 9-year-old, a teenager, and an adult. At each stage, she sings her son the same lullaby, even when she has to drive across town and climb a ladder to get into his bedroom window. Inevitably, the day comes when she is too old to hold him, and the roles are reversed: He drives across town, lifts her into his lap, and rocks her to sleep, singing his version of the lullaby.

Love Is a Special Way of Feeling by Joan Walsh Anglund. (1960). Harcourt. 32 pages. In this charming meditation on the wonders and special qualities of love, Joan Walsh Anglund describes the tender, happy feeling that is called love through poetic words and quaint illustrations of children. She goes beyond the typical bond between parents and children and provides a cheerful perspective of life's many pleasures.

On the Day You Were Born by Debra Frasier. (1991). Harcourt. 40 pages. Young children believe themselves to be the center of the world, and this book reinforces their conviction. With uncluttered, earth-toned collages, Debra Frasier explains how the earth celebrates the birth of a newborn baby: The sun, moon, tides, rain, trees, air, animals, and people of the world all work together to create a welcoming setting for the new baby's arrival. Older children will enjoy reading the detailed glossary, which explains the natural phenomena mentioned in the brief text, such as animal migration, falling rain, gravitational pull, growing trees, rising tides, rotation of the earth, and stellar constellations.

Just in Case You Ever Wondered by Max Lucado, illustrated by Toni Goffe. (1992). Tommy Nelson. 32 pages. A father tells his daughter how God made her especially for their family. The father promises that as the daughter gets older, he will always love her, hug her, and be on her side: She can always call for him or come to him for protection and comfort—no matter what happens. This tender message of love can provide encouragement and assurance to children that their parents love them and so does God, now and through eternity.

You Are My I Love You by Maryann K. Cuismano, illustrated by Satomi Ichikawa. (2001). Philomel. 32 pages. With rhyming verses and a multitude of similes, readers will share one day in the life and love of a parent and child. What makes this book unique is that the parent is a stuffed teddy bear and the child is a baby stuffed teddy bear who, interestingly, has an assortment of tiny stuffed animals that join in the child's daily activities. Throughout the book, the child is cheerful and capricious while the parent's watchful presence displays patience and wisdom. In this manner, the special connections between a parent and child are explored within the activities of a busy day of running, spinning, splashing, and hugging.

Concepts

The vast majority of best-selling concept books are in board book format, and they were introduced in the previous chapter. However, several longer concept books are published in regular formats that are appropriate for 3- and 4-year-olds.

Dr. Seuss's ABC by Dr. Seuss. (1963). Random House. 72 pages. Dr. Seuss's alphabet book is the top-selling alphabet book of all time, not only because of the popularity of the author but also because the book contains all of the essential components of a good alphabet book. It presents the letters in alphabetical order in both lower- and uppercase forms. One or more double-page spreads are devoted to each letter with engaging illustrations of several items that begin with the featured letter. Because vowels can represent many different sounds, good alphabet books show various items that start with the featured vowel's common sounds. Dr. Seuss is masterful in his examples for the letter *O*, ingeniously representing it in five ways: short vowel (*Oscar* and *ostrich*), long vowel (*only*), r-controlled vowel (*orange*), and both diphthong vowels—two vowel sounds in the same syllable (*oiled* and *owl*). Although most consonants represent only a single sound, there are a few exceptions. For example, *C* represents two common sounds, which Dr. Seuss exemplifies with *camel* and *ceiling*.

Chicka Chicka Boom Boom by Bill Martin Jr and John Archambault, illustrated by Lois Ehlert. (1989). Simon & Schuster. 40 pages. This delightful alphabet book deviates considerably from the norm because it does not match letters with sounds. Rather, it presents the alphabet in a rhyming story with strong rhythm. In a colorful tropical setting, the little alphabet letters represent playful children who decide to climb a coconut tree (in alphabetical order, of course). However, the tree cannot bear their weight, and as it bends to the ground the coconuts fall off, and then the little ones tumble after in a big heap. The capital letters (who represent the mamas, papas, uncles, and aunts) rush to their rescue. The little letters recover in amusing fashions:

Little *d* has a skinned knee (illustrated with some color missing from its front), *e* has a stubbed toe (illustrated with a swollen appendage), *f* wears a bandage, *h* is literally tangled up with *i*, and *p* is indeed black-eyed. As the sun goes down and a full moon appears, the indomitable little *a* leaps out of bed and double-dares his companions to another treetop race. In cut-paper collage, Lois Ehlert uses bold colors and hot pink and orange borders to match the lively mood of the verse.

Best Word Book Ever by Richard Scarry. (1963). Golden Books. 72 pages. In this pictorial vocabulary book, Richard Scarry presents 40 different concepts. Kenny and Kathy Bear and their Busytown friends introduce both familiar and new names for people, places, and objects that are grouped by subjects or settings. Some examples are the alphabet, colors, toys, games, tools, supermarket, mealtime, holidays, school, kitchen, cars and trucks, shapes and sizes, weather, seasons, bedtime, and numbers. The simple pictures give sufficient detail without overwhelming young children, and all have animal characters from Scarry's popular books. Scarry updated the illustrations in 1980 to give a more politically correct view of the world. For example, some of the community helpers such as police officers now wear skirts to show that the animal characters are female. This book can serve double duty, first as a way of developing young children's oral language and later as a means of developing sight-reading vocabulary.

Please and Thank You Book by Richard Scarry. (1973). Random House. 32 pages. This colorful book presents several vignettes in which the perky animal characters—such as Huckle, Lowly, Pig Will, and Pig Won't—of Busytown learn useful lessons about thoughtfulness, caring, and the good will generated by nice manners. The negative and positive examples of acting mannerly make this a fun book with which to learn social skills.

I Can Count to 100...Can You? by Katherine Howard. (1979). Random House. 32 pages. A colorful and cheerful mouse family introduces the numbers from 1 to 100 and invites children to count the cumulative sequences of toys, planes, animals, and other familiar objects. This book is a lively way to make learning the numbers beyond 10 (where most counting books end) easier to understand by demonstrating how the numbers 1 through 10 are repeated to make larger numbers.

Ten Little Rubber Ducks by Eric Carle. (2005). HarperCollins. 36 pages. This book does far more than present the counting numbers 1 through 10; it also introduces interesting concepts such as ordinal numbers (first, second, third, etc.) and the four geographical directions, as well as information on 10 different creatures in realistic habitats in various parts of the globe. When a giant wave washes a box of 10 little rubber ducks off a cargo ship, the ducks are swept away in various directions. The ducks bob along together for a while, but soon they drift in different directions, each encountering an animal, such as a dolphin, whale, seal, polar bear, and flamingo. As the sun sets, the 10th little rubber duck is left all alone, bobbing helplessly on the empty sea until she meets a mother duck with her ducklings, and she bobs along with them to their nest. When the ducks say their good night quacks, the little rubber duck replies, "Squeak." (Children can press a button on the page to hear a real squeaking noise.)

The Truck Book by Harry McNaught. (1978). Random House. 32 pages. This book traces the history of truck design (to include buses, campers, and fire engines) from the smallest and oldest to huge, more modern trucks. Not only does McNaught show readers what they look like, but he also explains how they have affected our world for its betterment. Some favorites include a giant dump truck with enormous wheels, a milk truck shaped like a bottle, an automobile carrier, a crane, and a forklift. After a few readings, children should be able to name the trucks they see driving by each day.

Seven Little Postmen by Margaret Wise Brown and Edith Thatcher Hurd, **illustrated by Tibor Gergely. (1952). Golden Books. 24 pages.** For every child who has wondered what happens after an envelope is dropped into a mailbox, this is an account of how one little boy's letter (about a litter of lively kittens) is delivered to his grandmother. Readers will see seven of the basic channels through which all mail must pass to be delivered to a distant location, and they will probably come to realize just how much time and effort is involved before a letter is delivered. The book is dated in its explanation of the machinery used in the process, and it makes no mention of zip codes because they first came into use after the book was published in 1952. In addition, many postal workers today are females, who are visibly absent in the book's text and illustrations. However, the book's popularity continues, as it also sparks an interest in children to write a letter to a loved one.

Traditional

Traditional literature, also called folk literature, consists of stories, songs, and rhymes with unknown authorship, which were passed down orally through generations long before they were ever written down. Each generation told these stories to the next, which in turn told the stories to the youth of the generation that followed, and each new storyteller made variations to the tales.

Because these stories and rhymes are in the public domain—that is, they are not copyrighted—they remain in a constant process of variation, and you can find a number of different published versions of each famous tale. So many versions of traditional tales and rhymes have been published, however, that few ever reach bestseller status. Yet, several traditional tales have won this acclaim, and I present them in the next section, followed by several best-selling collections of traditional rhymes.

Folktales

***The Little Red Hen* retold by Diane Muldrow, illustrated by J.P. Miller. (1954). Golden Books. 24 pages.** Children can learn a valuable lesson about teamwork from this funny, repetitive tale. When the Little Red Hen finds a grain of wheat and decides to plant it, none of the other animals will help her. When the wheat seed grows into a plant and bears many more grains of wheat, the Little Red Hen decides to makes some delicious bread. Before each step, she asks the other animals if any will help her, but they all quickly reply, "Not I." Her perpetual response is, "Then I will do it myself." When it comes time to eat the product of her lone labors, the cat, pig, duck, and goose all volunteer to help, but you guessed it—she does it all by herself.

***The Mitten: A Ukrainian Folktale* retold and illustrated by Jan Brett. (1989). Putnam. 32 pages.** Nicki is a Ukrainian boy whose grandmother Baba knits him some warm wool mittens. When he loses one of the white mittens in the snow, a mole takes refuge. Then a rabbit, hedgehog, owl, badger, and fox snuggle in. The animals are already packed in tightly when along comes a bear who manages to crawl in. However, a tiny mouse spoils the fun. When she squeezes in and her whiskers tickle the bear's nose, he sneezes, and all the animals fly out of their warm hiding place. Nicki spots his now enormous mitten and takes it home to show his Baba, who wonders how it became so stretched out. In Brett's signature style, intricate artwork is bordered with elaborate birch-bark designs that include embroidered details and mitten-shaped vignettes, providing additional insight into the story.

Who's That Knocking on Christmas Eve? retold and illustrated by Jan Brett. (2003). Grosset & Dunlap. 32 pages. In this traditional Norwegian folktale, every year trolls knock down the door of Kyri's hut and gobble up the holiday feast of sausages, fish, and tasty buns that she prepares for her father. However, this year, the trolls are in for a surprise. A cold, hungry boy and his pet ice bear (on their way to Oslo) have been invited into Kyri's hut, and the guests help to frighten away the greedy, long-snouted trolls who come to wreak havoc and steal the holiday treats. Once the hulking, heroic polar bear finishes with the trolls, they will not be returning. Intricately designed borders that frame the magnificent artwork reveal constellations studded with trolls, bears, and other Norwegian mythical symbols, romping through skies lit by northern lights.

Nursery Rhymes

Nursery rhymes are traditional verses intended for young children. Most of them are nonsensical, but that is part of their charm. They contain strong rhythm and alliterative language with action, humor, and entertaining incidents that make them attractive to children. Most likely, the nursery rhymes you heard as a child were of British origin and were called Mother Goose rhymes. Even though most nursery rhymes do not make sense today, historically they emerged from humorous verses that were based on real people, events, or customs. Some of the sources for the rhymes were old proverbs, street cries, games, ballads, and political satires.

The Real Mother Goose compiled and illustrated by Blanche Fisher Wright. (1916). Scholastic. 128 pages. Blanche Fisher Wright first published what is likely the best-known collection of nursery rhymes in 1916. Today, this comprehensive collection of over 300 rhymes is available through Scholastic, complete with its original Edwardian-style illustrations. In addition to perennial favorites such as "Humpty Dumpty," "Little Bo-Peep," "Pat-a-Cake," and "Three Blind Mice," many lesser known rhymes are included. To make them easier to locate, there is an alphabetic list of first lines at the beginning of the book. You may access the full text of this collection at the Project Gutenberg site (http://www.gutenberg.org/files/10607/10607.txt).

Mother Goose compiled and illustrated by Eloise Wilkin. (1920). Golden Books. 26 pages. Eloise Wilkin illustrated many of the early classic Golden Books, including *Prayers for Children*. In her short collection of nursery rhymes, she captures the timeless appeal of favorites such as "Baa, Baa, Black Sheep," "Georgie Porgie," "Jack and Jill," and "Little Miss Muffet."

Best Mother Goose Ever compiled and illustrated by Richard Scarry. (1964). Golden Books. 96 pages. I believe that Scarry's collection is more appropriate for today's youngsters than the previous collections listed. Instead of crowding as many rhymes as possible on each page, he gives each rhyme a double-page spread. Each of the collection's 50 rhymes is brightly illustrated with humorous animal characters. For example, Richard Scarry depicts the cow jumping over the moon in a pink dress and pearl necklace, and the little dog who laughs at her is wearing a sailor suit. Favorites include "Jack Sprat," "Old Mother Hubbard," "Peter Piper," and "Simple Simon."

Mother Goose compiled and illustrated by Aurelius Battaglia. (1973). Random House. 32 pages. Aurelius Battaglia colorfully illustrated this short collection of 36 favorite Mother Goose rhymes. In recent years, the rhymes in this and the other collections have been criticized for containing violence. I agree that a certain amount of violence in nursery rhymes and folktales originated from past cultures, and people today are more conscious of children's exposure to violence. However, Grover (1971) focused on the positive aspects of nursery rhymes, saying that "the healthy moral, so subtly suggested in many of the rhymes, is unconsciously absorbed by the child's receptive mind, helping him to make his own distinction between right and wrong, bravery and cowardice, generosity and selfishness" (p. 7).

Songs

Even the youngest of children enjoy listening to music and singing, and 3- and 4-year-olds are ready to learn the words and melodies. The following collections of traditional childhood songs are available as charmingly illustrated books with media included.

Wee Sing Children's Songs and Fingerplays by Pamela Conn Beall and Susan Hagen Nipp, illustrated by Nancy Spence Klein. (1977). Price Stern Sloan. 64 pages. This book and audio collection feature more than 70 traditional songs and fingerplays that will allow you to relive the fun of your own childhood by sharing the songs you grew up singing. Favorites include "Eentsy Weentsy Spider," "Hickory, Dickory Dock," "Where Is Thumbkin?" "Five Little Fishies," "This Old Man," "Down by the Station," "Bingo," "John Jacob Jingleheimer Schmidt," and "Old MacDonald Had a Farm." After listening a few times to the young voices singing on the accompanying recording, children should be able to pick up the words and music. (This provides a great diversion on long and short car trips when you pop the compact disc into your car stereo.)

Wee Sing and Play by Pamela Conn Beall and Susan Hagen Nipp, illustrated by Lisa Guida. (1981). Price Stern Sloan. 64 pages. The more than 70 songs in this collection are grouped by themes: choosing rhymes ("Eeny, Meeny, Miney, Mo"), circle and singing games ("The Farmer in the Dell"), jump rope rhymes ("Teddy Bear"), ball bouncing rhymes ("Pop! Goes the Weasel"), and clapping rhymes ("Head and Shoulders").

Wee Sing Silly Songs by Pamela Conn Beall and Susan Hagen Nipp, illustrated by Lisa Guida. (1982). Price Stern Sloan. 64 pages. Beall and Nipp feature 50 more songs for this collection, all sure to bring chuckles to children and adults alike, including "Michael Finnegan," "Do Your Ears Hang Low?" "The Bear Went Over the Mountain," "Little Bunny Foo Foo," "The Ants Go Marching," "Be Kind to Your Web-Footed Friends," "Found a Peanut," "There's a Hole in the Bucket," and "Ninety-Nine Bottles of Pop."

Realistic Fiction

Best-selling realistic books for young children are not common, although children will enjoy realistic fiction books if teachers, parents, and other caregivers select and share them. This is one reason why it is so important to balance children's reading selections, which is discussed further in chapter 7.

The Snowy Day by Ezra Jack Keats. (1962). Viking Press. 40 pages. Although he was not African American, Ezra Jack Keats broke ground when he published *The Snowy Day* in 1962. According to Brinson (1997), it was the first children's book published in the United States with an African American character portrayed in a nonstereotypical manner. The book is an account of a young boy who wakes to discover that snow has fallen during the night in his urban neighborhood. During his day of play, he experiments with footprints, knocks snow from a tree, creates snow angels, and tries to save a snowball for tomorrow. Much of the book's popularity was due to its winning the Caldecott Medal, the premier book award for illustrators, for Keats's innovative artwork, combining watercolor with collage.

***I'm a Big Sister* by Joanna Cole, illustrated by Maxie Chambliss. (1997). HarperCollins. 32 pages.** This book is for children who will soon be older siblings. It provides positive reinforcement on both the importance of being part of a family and on retaining one's individuality. The older sister tells how her family grows and changes when their new baby arrives, explaining what babies like, why they cry, and what they are not yet able to do (that she can do already). Not only does the book stress the joys of welcoming a new baby and the advantages of being the older child in the family, but it also focuses on how much the parents love all their children. In a concluding note to parents, the author offers suggestions on how to guide and reassure older children about the changes that are coming.

The companion book, *I'm a Big Brother*, contains identical text with the exception of substituting "brother" for "sister" throughout. Of course, the illustrations change the gender of the narrator as well. Although in the illustrations the sister entertains dolls at a tea party and the brother plays with trucks and building blocks, I encourage you to point out that those activities are appropriate for all children, regardless of gender. Another book with the same theme that features African American characters is *She Come Bringing Me That Little Baby Girl* by Eloise Greenfield and illustrated by John Steptoe.

***David Gets in Trouble* by David Shannon. (2002). Blue Sky Press. 32 pages.** In childlike paintings, a round-headed, sharp-toothed David (whose name ought to be Trouble-in-Progress) gives us a child's-eye view of the world where adults appear only as limbs and torsos. A series of snapshots shows David wreaking havoc in his house, and a childlike scrawl gives his reasoning, such as "I didn't mean to" (after skateboarding into a lamp table) and "It was an accident" (after hitting a baseball into a window). He also happily walks down the street in his underpants because he forgot his britches, pulls the cat's tail because she likes it, and stands next to a partially eaten chocolate cake, saying it wasn't *him*. At bedtime, however, David blurts out his guilt-ridden apology, saying it *was* him, and he is sorry. Yet, the reader knows the process will start again the next day, and David will have many more visits to the time-out corner.

Book cover from *The Little Engine That Could* retold by Watty Piper, illustrated by George Hauman and Doris Hauman. © 1930 by Platt & Munk. Used by permission of Penguin Group (http://www.penguin.com).

Chapter 5

Best-Selling Books for Children Ages 5–6

During the ages of 5 and 6, most children will learn to read. However, this does not mean you should stop reading to them. Remember that the majority of picture books are meant to be read *to* young children rather than *by* them. Just as children listened to books with enjoyment and comprehension before they learned to read, they will be able to enjoy and comprehend stories that are far above their emerging reading abilities when parents, teachers, and other caregivers read to them. Also, keep in mind that many younger children may be ready to listen to the books in this chapter before they are able to read them on their own.

I hope parents do not give away all the books they read to their children during the first five years of their lives because around age 6 the children will likely want to go back to those books and read them independently. If children heard the books often, they may have much of the text committed to memory and be able to predict what the words should be, thus reading the familiar stories more easily (Elizabeth Larkin, personal communication, November 1, 2005). Generally, emergent readers will quietly, but audibly, read to themselves. Of course, if there is a younger sibling around, he or she can benefit from listening to the older sibling. In fact, many children who start school knowing how to read have been taught by an older sibling.

The best-selling books for this age group are almost entirely animal fantasy. This does not mean that nearly all of the books published fall into this genre; the sales simply reflect that the majority of the books sold are animal fantasy. (Children should be exposed to a variety of literature, so I have addressed this issue in chapter 7, "Selecting Books to Supplement the Bestsellers.")

Easy–to–Read Books

In chapter 1, I talked about easy-to-read books that are specially designed for beginning readers. Though publishers have various trade names for their lines of easy-to-read books, they all have several characteristics in common:

- The books are smaller than regular picture books (typically about 6 inches by 9 inches).
- There are fewer illustrations and their relative size is smaller.
- A liberal amount of white space is achieved by larger print, more space between lines, and lines that do not run flush to the margin.
- Vocabulary is limited to fewer than 250 words, and most words contain only one syllable.
- Sentences are short and often have repeating text or rhyming lines.

Dr. Seuss

The Cat in the Hat by Dr. Seuss. (1957). Random House. 64 pages. The author with the most best-selling easy-to-read books is Dr. Seuss. In fact, *The Cat in the Hat* was the prototype of easy-to-read picture storybooks written on a beginning reader's level. Even though *The Cat in the Hat* has rhyming text, it is one of the more difficult books in this section, and many children will not be able to read it independently until they are in the middle of first grade. The story opens with a boy and his sister, Sally, who are bored sitting at home on a rainy afternoon. A cat wearing an odd red-and-white top hat appears, and with hilarious antics, he entertains the children with some balancing tricks. After he brings in his wild pals, Thing 1 and Thing 2, the house is a disaster, and the repeated admonitions of the fish in the bowl ring true. The mother is on the way home, and the children panic. However, the cat brings in a pick-up machine with multiple hands, and everything is amazingly put back in order before she steps inside.

The Cat in the Hat Comes Back by Dr. Seuss. (1958). Random House. 64 pages. In this sequel, snow rather than rain is spoiling the children's fun. Sally and her brother are grudgingly shoveling snow when the Cat in the Hat shows up. He lets himself inside and eats cake in their bathtub. When he gets out, he has left a big pink ring around the tub, which he decides to clean up with

Mother's white dress. The stubborn pink stain is then transferred from the dress to the wall, to Dad's shoes, and then to the rug in the hall. Finally, the cat calls for some assistance, and from inside his hat comes Little Cat A, who has Littler Cat B inside his hat, and so on through the alphabet as the ever-tinier cats, nested in ever tinier hats, pop out to clean everything up.

Green Eggs and Ham by Dr. Seuss. (1960). Random House. 64 pages. *Green Eggs and Ham* is Dr. Seuss's most popular book, and it is easy enough for a beginning reader to master. The vocabulary is very limited, picture clues are ample, and the repetitive and rhyming text enables readers to decode unfamiliar words. In this book, Sam-I-Am tries to convince another Seuss character to eat a plate of green eggs and ham. His persistence causes him to chase after the character, taking them both through a variety of settings and vehicles—house, box, tree, car, train, and boat. Finally, after the boat capsizes into the sea, the character agrees to taste the green eggs and ham to get rid of the tireless Sam-I-Am. He decides he likes them after all and would eat them anywhere and with anything—in a boat, with a goat, in the rain, on a train, in a box, with a fox, in a house, and with a mouse. (Perhaps this book could convince children to try a little spinach or another green vegetable.)

One Fish Two Fish Red Fish Blue Fish by Dr. Seuss. (1960). Random House. 64 pages. Only the first nine pages of this book are about fish. Thereafter, each spread has a silly verse about a funny and unusual Seuss character, such as a Wump with multiple humps, Ned in a too-short bed, a Nook with a cook book, a Zans who opens cans, a boxing Gox, a singing Ying, a hopping Yop, one-haired Zeds, a Yink who drinks pink ink, an Ish with a fish dish, a Gack with a rack of horns, and a pet Zeep with which to sleep. The multiple rhyming words (often several within each line of text) help children to master word families that have different beginning sounds but the same vowel and ending consonant.

Hop on Pop by Dr. Seuss. (1963). Random House. 64 pages. This is Seuss's simplest of books, making it appropriate for kindergartners to read independently. Each page has two monosyllabic rhyming words in large print, followed with a short (three- to five-word) sentence or two using the words in context. However, the sparse text is far from dull. The same is true for the nutty illustrations in which a child is as likely to bite a wild creature as to have one bite him. In addition to regular hardcover and paperback, this title is available in board book format.

Fox in Socks by Dr. Seuss. (1965). Random House. 64 pages. This book is a collection of amusing tongue twisters that Fox in Socks uses to tease his reluctant and exasperated friend Mr. Knox, such as telling him about the tweetle beetles who battle with paddles in a puddle. However, even though Mr. Knox complains that his tongue is not made from rubber, he does catch on before the end of the book (but do not be so sure that you will).

P.D. Eastman

Are You My Mother? by P.D. Eastman. (1960). Random House. 64 pages. While its mother is out looking for food, a baby bird bursts out of its shell. In looking for his mother, he falls out of the nest. Because he cannot fly, he sets off on a walking quest to find her. He asks everything that moves if it is his mother: kitten, hen, dog, cow, car, boat, airplane, and steam shovel (whom he calls "Snort"), but none of them is his mother. However, Snort returns him to his nest, where he is happily reunited with his mother after she flies back home with a juicy worm.

Go, Dog. Go! by P.D. Eastman. (1961). Random House. 64 pages. The text of this book of canine cartoons contains single-syllable words and rhythmic repetition combined into silly phrases that even a kindergartner can master (with help from the picture clues). Readers see many kinds of dogs in a variety of fun-filled activities that include driving little cars, skiing, and meeting new individuals. Particularly interesting is the slow-to-bud romance between the cheerful yellow dog and the perky pink poodle.

Peggy Parish

Amelia Bedelia by Peggy Parish, illustrated by Fritz Siebel. (1963). HarperTrophy. 64 pages. Peggy Parish was an educator who believed that children should learn to read with literature books instead of textbooks because children were not going to read with enthusiasm anything in which they were not interested. Her many books about Amelia Bedelia have helped children develop a positive attitude toward reading through many enjoyable and humorous hours. Amelia is a hardworking but simple maid who starts her first day of employment for the Rogers family with only a list of duties to complete before they return home. Even though it is not on the list, Amelia decides to bake one of her famous lemon meringue pies as a surprise, and then she studies the list carefully. Because Mrs. Rogers told her to do just what the list says, Amelia assumes a literal interpretation. When the list says to dust the furniture, she puts dusting powder on everything. When the list says to put the lights out, she hangs all the light bulbs on the clothesline for some fresh air. When the list says to dress the chicken, she sews some little green pants and socks to put on it. However, her pie is the best the Rogers have ever tasted, so they decide it makes up for Amelia's mistakes.

Merry Christmas, Amelia Bedelia by Peggy Parish, illustrated by Lynn Sweat. (1986). HarperTrophy. 64 pages. On Christmas Eve, Amelia Bedelia has to get the Rogers's house ready for a visit from Aunt Myra. She bakes a date cake by cutting up a calendar and including the tiny squares in the batter. She stuffs the children's stockings with turkey stuffing, and when told to pop six cups of popcorn, she uses six cups of kernels. The kitchen overflows with popped corn, but she manages to please Mrs. Rogers with fresh popcorn balls and Mr. Rogers with hot spice cake, so the holiday is saved.

Good Work, Amelia Bedelia by Peggy Parish, illustrated by Lynn Sweat. (1976). HarperTrophy. 64 pages. When Mr. and Mrs. Rogers go out for the day and leave a list of jobs for Amelia to do (will they never learn?), she handles them in her usual wacky way. Literal-minded Amelia pots the plants in cooking pots, patches the screen door with pieces of cloth from her sewing basket, and makes a sponge cake by adding to the batter cut-up pieces of the kitchen sponge. It is a good thing she also makes her famous butterscotch cake because that makes for a better desert.

Arnold Lobel

Frog and Toad Are Friends by Arnold Lobel. (1970). HarperTrophy. 64 pages. The four books in Arnold Lobel's Frog and Toad series have themes of unconditional friendship and sympathetic understanding. Frog and Toad live in little houses, wear human clothing, walk upright, eat human food, and are able to read and write. Because they live in an all-animal world, they are able to communicate with the other woodland creatures that, interestingly, live in natural habitats and do not wear clothing. Each book consists of five episodic chapters. In the first book, *Frog and Toad Are Friends*, my favorite chapter is "The Story."

Frog and Toad Together by Arnold Lobel. (1971). Harper Trophy. 64 pages.
My favorite chapter from the second book in the Frog and Toad series is "Cookies." When Toad bakes a bunch of delicious cookies, he takes them over to Frog's house. They find they cannot stop eating them and lack the willpower to stop. So, they put them in a box, tie it with string, and put it on a high shelf. When they realize all they have to do is climb a ladder to the shelf and untie the string to open the box to get the cookies, Frog takes the cookies outside and gives them to the birds, and Frog and Toad finally have willpower. The other two books in the series are equally good: *Frog and Toad All Year* and *Days With Frog and Toad*.

Else Holmelund Minarik

Little Bear by Else Holmelund Minarik, illustrated by Maurice Sendak. (1957). Harper Trophy. 64 pages. In five episodic chapters, readers learn of the deep caring that Mother Bear has for her playful son. When the weather is cold and snowy, Mother Bear makes a warm outfit for Little Bear to play in, but it turns out his own fur coat is best. Little Bear cannot find his mother and thinks she has forgotten his birthday, so he makes birthday soup for his guests, but of course before they eat the soup, Mother Bear shows up with a gorgeous cake. When Little Bear pretends to fly to the moon in his homemade space helmet, Mother Bear plays along but has a hot lunch waiting for him on his return. The gentle, teasing banter between Little Bear and his mother continue until bedtime when she recounts his activities in a bedtime story.

The four other books in the series are *Father Bear Comes Home*, *Little Bear's Friend*, *Little Bear's Visit*, and *A Kiss for Little Bear*.

Other Authors

Put Me in the Zoo by Robert Lopshire. (1960). Random House. 64 pages.
Spot is a polka-dotted leopard who can change colors and even juggle his own spots. He insists that he belongs in the zoo because of his talents, but the zoo will not take him. After the zoo security guards toss him out, Spot demonstrates his special abilities to two children. He makes his spots bigger and then smaller, and he even places them on the boy. However, the children suggest a better

place for Spot and lead him to the circus, where he learns that it is best to capitalize on inherent traits rather than changing to suit what others may want. (In the last scene, look for the Cat in the Hat in the audience, watching Spot perform at the circus.)

Danny and the Dinosaur by Syd Hoff. (1958). Harper Trophy. 64 pages. When Danny goes to the museum to see the displays, he is more than a little surprised when one of the dinosaurs comes to life (after 100 million years) and agrees to play with him outside. The lovable dinosaur spends the day with Danny and his friends in the middle of town, where a dinosaur comes in handy, serving as a bridge across a busy street. However, playing hide–and–seek does present a few problems. Some of their other adventures include a visit to the ballpark and the zoo.

A Fly Went By by Mike McClintock, illustrated by Fritz Siebel. (1958). Random House. 64 pages. A young boy is resting in a boat by the lake when he sees a fly whiz by, followed by a frog that is chased by a cat, which is chased by a dog and a host of other frantic characters in this humorous cumulative tale. Each fleeing character is fearful that a larger animal is trying to catch him, but only the child is fearless enough to confront each animal in turn to get to the root of their fears—nothing but a little sheep whose back hoof was caught in a tin can, making it thump and bump and scare everyone.

Jack and Jill and Big Dog Bill by Martha Weston. (2002). Random House. 32 pages. The Jack and Jill in this book go up the hill but not to fetch a pail of water. They intend to sled down the snowy hill with their big dog named Bill. However, each time they are poised at the top and ready to go, a rabbit distracts Bill, and comical chaos results on the downhill run. The author makes liberal use of alliteration, rhyming, and repetition to ensure that the youngest of readers can be successful reading this book.

A Fish Out of Water by Helen Palmer, illustrated by P.D. Eastman. (1961). Random House. 72 pages. A young boy goes to a pet store and buys a little goldfish, which he names Otto. The storeowner, Mr. Carp, cautions him not to overfeed it. However, when the fish still appears to be hungry, the boy starts giving him more food, and Otto begins to grow. First, he outgrows his fish bowl and then a vase. When Otto keeps growing, the boy puts him in a large cook pot and then the bathtub, but even that becomes too small. After the boy calls the fire department, men tow poor Otto in a truck and, using a crane, they drop him into a large swimming pool, but soon Otto is too big for even that. Mr. Carp is called, and he magically shrinks Otto back to his normal size. When he tells the boy that Otto can only be given just a spot of food, we know this time the boy will follow the advice.

The Little Engine That Could retold by Watty Piper, illustrated by George Hauman and Doris Hauman. (1930). Platt & Munk. 40 pages. In a great tale of motivation and the power of positive thinking, a little train is confronted with an almost insurmountable task. A train carrying loads of nutritious food and talking toys for all of the good children in the next town becomes stranded. The toys try to find another engine to help, but they cannot convince the shiny new engine, the big strong engine, or the tired old engine to pull them over the mountain. Only the Little Blue Engine agrees to try, chanting the rallying mantra of "I think I can, I think I can...." Her persistence saves the day, and she serves as an inspiration for all the readers who face difficult tasks.

Animal Fantasy in an All–Animal World

The rest of the books in this chapter do not have all the characteristics of easy-to-read books, but they are appropriate for 5- and 6-year-olds.

The most popular type of animal fantasy is set in a world that contains no humans, only animals that can think and talk like humans. This imaginary world may be inhabited by a single species such as the bears in Stan and Jan Berenstain's books, or it may be a world inhabited by various species such as Marc Brown's Arthur series. The animals may retain many of their natural traits such as the characters in books by Eric Carle. On the other hand, they may act entirely like humans, in which case the plots involve the same problems encountered by real children, whose lives these animals reflect. Sometimes only the illustrations reveal to readers that the characters are animals and not people.

Eric Carle

The Very Hungry Caterpillar by Eric Carle. (1969). Philomel. 28 pages. A tiny, hungry caterpillar pops from a little egg on a Sunday morning, and readers follow him through each day of the week as he tries to satisfy his enormous appetite. At the end of the week, after eating through one apple, two pears, three plums, four strawberries, five oranges, and 10 pieces of junk food, he is neither tiny nor hungry. He spins a little brown house around himself, sleeps for a few weeks, and through the miracle of metamorphosis, he becomes a beautiful butterfly. In Carle's unique style, the book contains pages of differing sizes with die cuts to represent holes where the caterpillar has eaten through the food. Not only do all of Carle's books have innovative formats, but they also contain exceptionally sturdy pages. His signature style of artwork is beautifully created by collage, using cut pieces of transparent tissue papers, which he has lightly streaked with paints.

The Very Quiet Cricket by Eric Carle. (1990). Philomel. 28 pages. *The Very Quiet Cricket* was the first book in which Eric Carle embedded a fiber-optic microchip with a light sensor (powered by a built-in replaceable battery) that makes a sound or flashes lights when the page is opened. In this book, a newly hatched cricket tries to answer the various animals that greet him, such as the big cricket, locust, cicada, and spittlebug, but he is unable to make a sound when he rubs his wings like the other crickets. Finally, as night falls, he meets a quiet little she-cricket, and he is so joyful that he makes his first chirping sound (on the last page of the book). Although the cricket sound is electronic, it is realistic. (So realistic, says kindergarten teacher Carolyn Eichenberger, she once searched all over the room for a cricket until she noticed some children looking at the book.)

The Grouchy Ladybug by Eric Carle. (1977). Philomel. 44 pages. A ladybug becomes grouchy after landing on a leaf containing juicy aphids, and she discovers that another ladybug got there first. The grouchy ladybug tries to pick fights with 12 progressively larger animals. The pages and the print become progressively larger with the sizes of the animals, and a clock in the upper left-hand corner of the pages shows the passing hours of the day. The final animal, a whale, is nine pages long, and children can flip the die-cut tail back and forth, showing how the whale slaps the ladybug back to land. Finally, a wet, tired, and very hungry ladybug ends up on the leaf where her sojourn started, and the original ladybug shares the rest of the aphids with her.

Mister Seahorse by Eric Carle. (2004). Philomel. 32 pages. Mrs. Seahorse carefully lays her eggs on Mr. Seahorse's belly, and he conveys them around in his pouch until they hatch. As he happily carries his brood, he meets other male fish who similarly bear the burden of prenatal care: the stickleback, tilapia, nursery fish, pipefish, and bullhead catfish. Interspersed between these encounters are scenes where Mr. Seahorse swims past camouflaged marine creatures, such as a trumpet fish that is hiding in reeds. Hidden creatures are revealed when readers turn the colorful overlaying acetate pages. Finally, Mr. Seahorse's task is complete, and the babies hatch and swim away on their own (after a little urging from their father). The multicolored fish and translucent scenery evoke a peaceful oceanic setting.

Stan and Jan Berenstain

At last count, the husband and wife author–illustrator team have published 54 books in their Berenstain Bears series, 39 of which have become all-time best-selling children's books. As I have with other series, I include only their top three books and leave the rest for you to discover on your own.

The Berenstain Bears' New Baby by Stan and Jan Berenstain. (1974). **Random House. 32 pages.** When Small Bear outgrows the bed his father made him when he was a baby, they go into the woods to cut a tree, so Papa Bear can make him a bigger bed. When Small Bear asks what will happen to his little bed, Papa tells him that they will very soon have a new baby. (It appears Small Bear had not noticed that Mama Bear had grown very round lately—only that he could not fit on her lap anymore.) At the end of the day, they return home with Small Bear's newly built bed, and the new baby (who apparently arrived with no assistance) is sleeping in the little bed that is now in his parents' bedroom. Small Bear happily accepts Baby Bear into the family.

The Berenstain Bears and the Messy Room by Stan and Jan Berenstain. (1983). Random House. 32 pages. The room shared by Brother and Sister Bear is a mess because the cubs argue over who should straighten up instead of working together. Mama Bear loses her temper and starts tossing things into a big trash box. When Papa Bear hears the crying, he thinks of a solution. He builds a big toy box and a pegboard, and Mama and the cubs categorize the toys into boxes that are labeled and put neatly into the closet. After the entire Bear family works together, the cubs' room stays clean and organized.

The Berenstain Bears Go to School by Stan and Jan Berenstain. (1978). **Random House. 32 pages.** Sister Bear is nervous about entering kindergarten, but her mother takes her to meet the teacher, and Sister Bear decides that school might be fun. However, when the first day of school starts, Brother Bear must nudge her along. The bus ride is a bit scary when all of the bigger kids get on and talk loudly, but Sister Bear overcomes her fears when she discovers all there is to do at school: paint pictures, build with blocks, play with clay, look at books, have a snack and a nap, and listen to stories. It turns out that school really is fun.

Other popular books in the series include *The Berenstain Bears Meet Santa Bear*, *The Berenstain Bears and Too Much Junk Food*, and *The Berenstain Bears and Too Much TV*.

Marc Brown

***Arthur's Birthday* by Marc Brown. (1989). Random House. 32 pages.** Arthur is a young, bespectacled aardvark who excitedly anticipates his birthday party because all of his relatives are coming from Ohio. He happily hands out invitations to his classmates, but he is dismayed when he learns that Muffy has scheduled a party for the same time and her parents have already booked a rock band and Pickles the clown. Their friends reluctantly take sides, even though they wish they could go to both parties. However, Arthur and Francine decide to forge Muffy's handwriting on new invitations, changing the location of her party to Arthur's house. The unsuspecting Muffy is lured there by the promise of a present too big to fit in her mailbox. The gift is a surprise party, which is heartily enjoyed by all the children together.

***Arthur's Reading Race* by Marc Brown. (1996). Random House. 32 pages.** Arthur does not believe that his little sister D.W. can really read, so he challenges her to prove it. Arthur promises to buy ice cream for her if she can read 10 words. They race to the park, where D.W. is quick to recognize signs with the words *Zoo*, *Don't walk*, *Police*, and *Ice cream*. She also reads *Wet paint* before her big brother does, and Arthur gets paint on his britches. This is a fabulous book for getting emergent readers interested in identifying environmental print.

***Arthur's Back to School Surprise* by Marc Brown. (1996). Random House. 32 pages.** Arthur, little sister D.W., and their mother go shopping for school supplies, and both children end up buying identical backpacks. On the first day of school, Arthur opens his backpack, and D.W.'s talking toy, Mary Moo-Cow, falls out in front of all of his friends. To Arthur's embarrassment, they begin to laugh and tease him.

Animal Fantasy in a Human World

In some animal fantasy stories, animals coexist with humans. This can be in a human-dominated world, as in *Clifford the Big Red Dog*, in which the animals may or may not be able to speak. Other times the setting is an animal-dominated world in which humans only occasionally appear, as in *The Story of Babar*.

Where the Wild Things Are by Maurice Sendak. (1963). HarperCollins. 44 pages. Max is wearing his wolf suit and making mischief of one kind or another (including chasing the dog with a spear-like fork in his hand), so he is reprimanded for his wild behavior and sent to his room without supper. There, a forest grows with an ocean tumbling by, and Max sails to the land of the Wild Things, which are big creatures (depicted with body parts from various animals, including humans) with sharp teeth, long claws, and silly grins on their faces. Because he tames them, they make him king of all Wild Things, and a wild rumpus ensues throughout the jungle. When Max gets lonely, he sails back the way he came, and his supper is waiting for him in his room. In this enchanted journey, Maurice Sendak shows the passage of time by the moon first seen through the bedroom window: When Max leaves, it is a quarter moon, but when he returns, it is a full moon, proving that his experiences were not just a dream.

Make Way for Ducklings by Robert McCloskey. (1941). Viking Press. 32 pages. Mr. and Mrs. Mallard fly over Boston, Massachusetts, looking for a good home to raise a family. They set down on a little island in the pond at the Public Garden, and they love the peanuts people throw to them. However, many rowdy children are around, so they move on to a place near the banks of the Charles River. There, Mrs. Mallard makes her nest and lays eight eggs, which she faithfully keeps warm until they hatch. While she is teaching the ducklings—Jack, Kack, Lack, Mack, Nack, Ouack, Pack, and Quack—how to walk in a straight line and how to swim and dive, Mr. Mallard goes exploring downriver. The excitement comes when Mrs. Mallard decides to lead her eight little hatchlings from the river to the Public Garden, and Michael the police officer must step in to stop cars so that the duck family can safely pass and meet Mr. Mallard at the little island in the pond. Every year, this book is reenacted in Boston's Public Gardens.

Blueberries for Sal by Robert McCloskey. (1948). Viking Press. 54 pages. Little Sal and her mother set off in search of blueberries to preserve for winter at the same time a mother bear and her cub go looking for berries to fatten up before winter. As the pairs proceed up opposite sides of the hill, each mother is focusing on her targeted task, thinking of the harsh winter ahead. However, Little Sal and the bear cub are intent on eating as many blueberries as they can find, and they wander away and lose sight of their mothers. Little Sal hears the mother bear and starts to wander in her direction at the same time that Little Bear hears the human mother and does the same. Eventually, the mothers discover the mistake, back away in shyness from the other's child, and find their own young ones to take safely home.

Curious George by H.A. Rey, illustrated by Margret Rey. (1941). Random House. 32 pages. The man with the big yellow hat captures a curious little monkey in Africa and calls him George. The man takes George on a big ship across the ocean (which George falls into while trying to fly like a seagull) to his home in a big U.S. city. Though George does not talk, he is able to understand human speech. He can also do everything humans can although he invariably bungles the activity, such as using the telephone and accidentally calling the fire department, which lands him in prison. He escapes from prison and flies over the city with balloons. The man in the big yellow hat finds George atop a traffic light, and—after paying for the balloons—he takes George to live in a zoo. However, in the many books about George that follow, George lives with the man.

Curious George Makes Pancakes by Vipah Interactive. (1998). Houghton Mifflin. 64 pages. After the deaths of H.A. and Margret Rey, Vipah Interactive, animators and producers of the Curious George CD-ROMs, created eight more Curious George books, using a similar style of art. The most popular of the books in the new series is *Curious George Makes Pancakes*. At the annual pancake breakfast fundraiser for the children's hospital, George decides to help. He begins adding blueberries to the pancakes, and the line for them becomes so long that the cook has to go for more help. The cook is furious when he returns to find that a monkey is making his pancakes, and he chases George through the other events at the fundraiser. However, all is forgiven when George raises so much money at the dunk tank that he is given the honor of presenting the money to the president of the hospital.

Clifford the Big Red Dog by Norman Bridwell. (1963). Cartwheel. 32 pages. Clifford the Big Red Dog is *really* big—taller than his owner's house. In the first book of the series, readers learn that Clifford must be bathed in a swimming pool and combed with a rake, and he generally wreaks havoc on the neighborhood. He chases cars (and catches them), digs up trees, and chews on store signs. However, having a giant dog has its advantages. When his owner, Emily Elizabeth, goes camping, Clifford serves as a tent, and he is an excellent watchdog: The bad boys do not come around anymore—that's for sure!

Clifford the Small Red Puppy by Norman Bridwell. (1972). Cartwheel. 32 pages. Clifford begins life as a runt—a very small red puppy—but Emily Elizabeth wishes that he would grow up to be big and strong, not small and sick like his breeder said he would be. One day, Mother and Emily Elizabeth notice that Clifford does seem bigger. His collar and sleeping basket are too small, and he soon outgrows Emily's bed as well. When Clifford grows too big to get out the door of the house, a crane has to lift him into a moving van that takes him to the country to live with Emily Elizabeth's uncle. They miss each other so much that Daddy gets a new job working with her uncle, and they all move to the country.

Clifford's Happy Easter by Norman Bridwell. (1994). Cartwheel. 32 pages. Emily Elizabeth and her big red dog Clifford love springtime, especially Easter. Her parents provide an enormous quantity of eggs for her to color, but she has a few problems. Because of Clifford's size, he crushes more eggs than he decorates, and he falls into the vat of dye for the eggs. When Emily Elizabeth falls asleep that night, she has a funny dream in which Clifford changes into many colors and designs.

The Very Lonely Firefly by Eric Carle. (1995). Philomel. 28 pages. A newly hatched firefly is seeking others of his kind. He is attracted to a variety of lights, such as a lightbulb, candle, flashlight, lantern, headlights, and fireworks. A subplot is conveyed through the illustrations of a family seeking the source of loud noises, which turn out to be a display of beautiful fireworks. After the fireworks are over, the very lonely firefly finally finds other fireflies, and when readers turn the last page, eight little fireflies blink on and off via tiny lightbulbs powered by a built-in replaceable battery.

***Click, Clack, Moo: Cows That Type* by Doreen Cronin, illustrated by Betsy Lewin. (2000). Simon & Schuster. 32 pages.** Farmer Brown hears "click, clack, moo" from the barn and discovers that his cows are using an old typewriter they found there. They send him a typed demand for better working conditions: It is too cold in the barn, and they want electric blankets. When he refuses to comply, they go on strike, and the chickens join them—no milk or eggs until their demands are met. With the help of an impartial mediator, a duck, they finally reach an agreement; however, the ducks confiscate the typewriter and make their own demands.

***Giggle, Giggle, Quack* by Doreen Cronin, illustrated by Betsy Lewin. (2002). Simon & Schuster. 32 pages.** In this sequel to *Click, Clack, Moo*, Duck has moved from collective bargaining to subterfuge. Farmer Brown is going on vacation, and he asks his brother Bob to take care of the animals, warning him to keep an eye on Duck, who is a troublemaker. Bob follows the instructions in Farmer Brown's notes exactly, but Duck has changed the notes to things such as ordering pizza with anchovies for the hens, bathing the pigs with bubble bath, and letting the cows choose a movie for the evening ("The Sound of Moosic"). Well-meaning, but oblivious, Bob pampers the barnyard critters, but the scam ends when Farmer Brown calls to check on things and hears "Giggle, giggle, quack" in the background, while the animals are happily lolling on the sofa, making themselves quite at home in Farmer Brown's living room.

***Dream Snow* by Eric Carle. (2000). Philomel. 32 pages.** It is almost Christmas, but there is no snow. Meanwhile, a white-bearded farmer falls asleep in his favorite chair after drinking peppermint tea, and he dreams of his animals—named One, Two, Three, Four, and Five—being covered in a gentle blanket of new snow. Acetate pages printed with snow overlay each of the following pages, concealing the animals until readers lift them to discover in turn the horse, cow, sheep, pig, and rooster. When the farmer awakens, he discovers that real snow has fallen, so he bundles up in his warm red suit and hurries out to decorate his tree. After strewing gifts for all five animals under the tree, the farmer shouts "Merry Christmas" and pushes a button to play a yuletide jingle. Readers who push the book's real button will turn on a microchip that plays a tinkling holiday tune. Illustrations are in Carle's trademark textured collages with rich colors that capture the snowy magic of Christmastime.

Poetry

With the exception of Mother Goose rhymes, which were included with traditional literature in the previous chapter, books of poetry are rare among best-selling children's books. However, three classic books are very popular and include a narrative poem and two short collections by a classic author.

The Night Before Christmas attributed to Clement C. Moore, illustrated by Mary Engelbreit. (1912). HarperCollins. 32 pages. Many beautiful versions of this classic narrative poem are in print, such as those illustrated by Robert Sabuda (in a beautiful and complex pop-up version), Jan Brett, and Christian Birmingham. Mary Engelbreit's interpretation of this poem features rambunctious elves who accompany the jolly St. Nicholas. He leaves assorted old-fashioned candies and toys inside a cozy and comfortable home on Christmas Eve where a mouse is asleep in its snug little den and children are dreaming as sugarplum fairies flutter around their bed.

"The Night Before Christmas" is one of the most widely read poems in the world, and it has been credited with creating the U.S. image of Santa Claus. The poem was first published anonymously in 1823 in *The Troy Sentinel*. Recently, the literary world was shocked when Don Foster, an English professor and internationally renowned scholar of authorial attribution at Vassar College, announced that after careful research, he was certain that Henry Livingston, Jr. wrote the beloved poem—not Clement C. Moore. Foster explained that more than 20 years after the poem first appeared in print and Livingston had passed away, Moore took credit for the poem by including it in a collection of his typically somber and pious poems (see Kirkpatrick, 2000).

When We Were Very Young by A.A. Milne, illustrated by Ernest H. Shepard. (1924). Dutton. 112 pages. *When We Were Very Young*, the first of A.A. Milne's four renowned books for children, introduces his son, Christopher Robin. Though its popularity is not as strong as it once was, during the 20th century, this book was likely read more often than any other book of children's verses. It charmingly reflects the experiences of a little English boy and his friends (some imaginary) in the early 1900s as he learns about the growing complexity of his world. Though much of the language is dated, and the customs may be unfamiliar to modern readers, children can still take delight in hearing about the changing of the guard at Buckingham Palace, the importance of staying in the squares when walking down the street, the disappearance of James-James's mother, the three foxes without sockses, and why Christopher Robin goes hoppity hop everywhere. Readers get their first glimpse of the tubby little stuffed bear that Christopher Robin sleeps with in the poem "Teddy Bear." However, the toy's name is Mr. Edward Bear in the poem. In a later book, the beloved bear is called Pooh. Ernest H. Shepard's illustrations in this and the other three books by Milne are based on the real toys that the author's son played with.

Now We Are Six by A.A. Milne, illustrated by Ernest H. Shepard. (1927). **Dutton. 101 pages.** In the foreword to this book, Milne explained that the poems in his second collection were written during the span of years when Christopher Robin was ages 3–6 (and thus the title). In the poem "Us Two," Christopher has now given the name of Pooh to his companion, a stuffed teddy bear. Wherever Christopher goes, whether for tutoring in the nursery or around the grounds looking for dragons, Pooh is his constant companion. In the poem "The Engineer," readers get their first view of the rest of the toys that are characters in Milne's next two books: Piglet, Kanga, Roo, and Eeyore. (Tigger is noticeably absent.)

Visual Games

Do you remember the old game of "I spy something in this room, and it is...," which is followed by a description that gets increasingly more detailed until the other person can guess what the item is? Visual game books are like the I Spy game, except they are exceedingly more elaborate and entertaining. Children can sharpen their visual acuity skills and even learn simple categorization if an adult will provide a prompt, for example, "Name all the things that are yellow (round/tiny/living) on this page."

Where's Waldo? by Martin Handford. (1987). Candlewick. 32 pages.
Waldo, wearing a red-and-white striped shirt and hat and blue pants, is hiking around the world. He visits many crowed areas where viewers are invited to search for him in the expansive, detailed illustrations, which are teeming with people from every lifestyle and contain many humorous vignettes. However, Waldo is not traveling alone; his dog, Woof, who is outfitted in a red-and-white striped sweater that extends to the end of his tail (and only his tail is ever visible), accompanies him. In every scene, viewers can search for additional characters, such as Wenda (whose attire is similar to Waldo's but with a blue skirt instead of pants), Wizard Whitebeard (who carries a red, white, and blue staff and is dressed in a red caftan and blue hat), and Odlaw (outfitted in black and yellow stripes). Additionally, 25 different Waldo-watchers appear once in the book and are recognizable because they wear a red-and-white striped shirt similar to Waldo's and Wenda's. Not only are there people to search for, but also Waldo's key, Woof's bone, Wenda's camera, Wizard Whitebeard's scroll, and Odlaw's binoculars are concealed within the details of each illustration (not necessarily near their owners).

Long after viewers have found Waldo and friends in each scene, there is still much to enjoy on every page, and each visit reveals something new. In addition to developing visual acuity and categorization skills, children can develop their visual literacy with this book. Visual literacy—the ability to interpret graphic stimuli—is practiced when children look carefully at the many small vignettes within each of the large illustrations and tell what might be happening. For example, children might say, "Three people are washing windows at the top of a building, and one of them has accidentally dropped a bucket of water. It looks like it is going to fall on a man walking on the sidewalk, who is dressed in a suit. I think he is going to get very angry because he is probably on his way to work."

I Spy: A Book of Picture Riddles by Jean Marzollo, illustrated by Walter Wick. (1992). Cartwheel. 40 pages. Rhyming riddles send readers searching for hundreds of small objects that are concealed within large photographs presented on 13 double-page spreads. Each of the photographs is themed, for example, arts and crafts, at the beach, blocks, make believe, nature, round things, and toy chest. Objects range from large and easy-to-spot to tiny and partially hidden. Just a few of the interesting things that viewers are looking for include a baby's footprint, heart-shaped box, silver jack, train track, comb, button, and pine cone. Children will delight in finding something new every time they view the book, and after they solve the initial riddles, readers can check out the extra riddles in the back and read suggestions for countless other games to play with the book.

I Spy Christmas: A Book of Picture Riddles by Jean Marzollo, illustrated by Walter Wick. (1993). Cartwheel. 40 pages. *I Spy Christmas* follows the same format as the previous book, except that each colorful spread explores a different aspect of the Christmas holiday: ornaments, winter wonderland, window shopping, holly and ivy, winter sports, cookie baking, Christmas crafts, Santa's workshop, stocking stuffers, teddy bears, nutcracker sweets, under the tree, and "Silent Night." Items range from large and obvious to subtle and partially hidden. In the back are instructions on how to create your own riddles after children have memorized the locations of all the objects named in the text.

I Spy Treasure Hunt by Jean Marzollo, illustrated by Walter Wick. (1999). Cartwheel. 40 pages. Although Jean Marzollo and Walter Wick published many books in their I Spy series, *I Spy Treasure Hunt* and the previous two are their most popular. In *I Spy Treasure Hunt*, readers once again study the beautifully composed photographs to search for subtly concealed objects. The illustrations in this book differ from the others because the photographs are of charming three-dimensional dioramas that depict scenes from a quaint seaside town. Children will pursue the mystery of the pirate's hidden treasure by solving the riddle on each delightful page. Marzollo and Wick also include information on how the sets for this pictorial treasure hunt were built and photographed.

Can You See What I See? by Walter Wick. (2002). Candlewick. 40 pages. With his signature style of artwork, Walter Wick presents 12 enticing photographs filled with a fascinating assortment of objects that one might find in a jumbled toy chest: blocks, beads, robots, dice, marbles, plastic animals, cards, and board game pieces. The clever rhyming text challenges readers with lists of items to find, but this book contains more than just hunt-and-find exercises. The text on each spread ends with a twist that requires readers to go back in the book to solve brain-teasing puzzles, such as following an alphabet maze, identifying robot parts, and matching 10 broken toys to their 10 missing pieces. At the end of the book, the author describes his work and provides some puzzle-solving hints.

Concepts

Most of the best-selling concept books are more appropriate for younger children. However, Graeme Base has written two that are of interest to older children because of their elaborate designs, sophisticated words, and visual games.

Animalia **by Graeme Base. (1986). Harry N. Abrams. 32 pages.** *Animalia* is far more than just an alphabet book featuring remarkably illustrated animals. Each letter of the alphabet has one or two pages devoted to elaborate and gorgeous illustrations of countless things that begin with the featured letter. For example, on the *L* page, in addition to *lazy lions*, viewers find *lace, ladder, ladle, lamb, lamp, Land Rover, Lassie the dog, lantern, lattice work, law books, leaves, lemon, leopard, leprechaun, lettuce, library, lightning, lilies, literature, lizard, llama, lobster, lock, locomotive, log, Lone Ranger, lyre*, and more. Each letter also presents an intricate tongue twister using the name of the featured animal with as many as seven other words that begin with that letter—all in a phrase that describes the scene. In addition, each page has a hidden picture of the illustrator as a child (though sometimes only a piece of him, such as a hand, is showing). Base spent three years completing the artwork for this extraordinary book, first published in Australia, which became an international bestseller.

The Water Hole **by Graeme Base. (2001). Harry N. Abrams. 32 pages.** *The Water Hole* is a counting book that is a companion to *Animalia*. It features animals from several continents who gather at a water hole deep in the forest: one rhinoceros, two tigers, three toucans, and so on—through 10 kangaroos. Die-cut pages reveal the water hole in 10 different habitats, such as the African plains, Himalayan Mountains, and Australian outback. As readers turn the pages, and the number of animals at the water hole increases, the amount of water diminishes (as does the number of water-frolicking frogs) until eventually there is nothing but dry, cracked earth. (Perhaps the water hole symbolizes world resources, especially the shrinking habitats of near-extinct animals.) Finally, a single drop of rain splatters on the parched soil. Then it rains until all the animals return to the replenished water hole. Younger children will enjoy an enchanting counting book filled with familiar creatures, but older children will discover nearly 100 hidden animals—some of them endangered—that appear in shadows within the landscapes and in the borders of the illustrations.

BY CHARLES TAZEWELL

The Littlest Angel

ILLUSTRATED BY

PAUL MICICH

Book cover from *The Littlest Angel* by Charles Tazewell, illustrated by Paul Micich. Text ©
1946 by the author and renewed by Louise Tazewell. Illustrations © by Ideals Children's
Books, publisher (http://www.idealsbook.com, 1–800–586–2572). ISBN 08249–5332–0.

Chapter 6

Best-Selling Books for Children Ages 7–8

Children ages 7 and 8 should be able to read the books in this chapter independently, but most will still love to have you read to them each day. (Also, keep in mind that many younger children may be ready to listen to these books before they learn to read them on their own.) When children are around 8 years old, they usually begin to read juvenile novels and chapter books in addition to picture books. Therefore, this chapter is shorter than the preceding ones.

Fantasy is still very popular with children ages 7 and 8, but their interests branch out beyond animal fantasy to other types of fantasy with a variety of human characters. In addition, children develop an interest in realistic books with characters that have no magical qualities. Nonfiction also becomes appealing to the children in this age group, although younger children will enjoy nonfiction if teachers and parents share good books with them (see Mohr, 2006). For children to succeed in school, it is essential for them to become familiar with a variety of text structures. I encourage teachers and parents to follow the lead of researchers who "are now interested in looking beyond stories to consideration of a variety of informational text formats" (Connor & Tiedemann, 2005, p. 12). Because of the many learning opportunities to be gained from intriguing informational books, I have included some additional nonfiction titles in chapter 7.

Animal Fantasy

The majority of the 200 best-selling children's picture books are picture storybooks, and because animal fantasy is the most popular genre with young children, it is fitting that the very first picture storybook was animal fantasy. *The Tale of Peter Rabbit* by Beatrix Potter was published by Frederick Warne & Co. in 1902. Before *Peter Rabbit*, book illustrations served only as decorations. Beatrix Potter was the first to match her illustrations with the text, using the pictures to share in the storytelling process, thus making *Peter Rabbit* the prototype of modern picture storybooks. In this and her 22 other books that followed, Potter used watercolors to illustrate woodland animals dressed as ordinary country folk.

The Tale of Peter Rabbit by Beatrix Potter. (1902). Frederick Warne & Co. 64 pages. Beatrix Potter was the daughter of a wealthy lawyer in London, England, and her parents raised her in seclusion, allowing her no contact with children other than her younger brother. The servants and governesses who cared for her sneaked small field animals to her nursery room to be her playmates. These animals became the characters in the beloved stories she wrote and illustrated, the first of which was *The Tale of Peter Rabbit*. This cautionary tale warns children about the consequences of not minding their parents. Peter is in jeopardy of losing his life when Mr. McGregor finds him nibbling vegetables in his garden and narrowly escapes, but he loses his new blue jacket and little shoes. After he returns home exhausted, his mother puts him to bed with a dose of chamomile tea, but his compliant sisters, Flopsy, Mopsy, and Cotton-tail, are rewarded with bread, milk, and delicious blackberries for supper.

The Tale of Peter Rabbit ranks among the top four all-time best-selling children's picture books in the United States. Additionally, in the United Kingdom, Beatrix Potter ranked second—after Ernest Hemingway—as the favorite author of all time in a poll conducted by the United Kingdom Library Association (International Reading Association, 2002/2003).

The Tale of Benjamin Bunny by Beatrix Potter. (1904). Frederick Warne & Co. 64 pages. The sequel to *The Tale of Peter Rabbit* is *The Tale of Benjamin Bunny* in which Peter and his cousin Benjamin sneak back to Mr. McGregor's garden to retrieve Peter's clothes, which are being used on a scarecrow. Though Peter wants to retrieve his clothing, he is fearful that Mr. McGregor will return from his buggy ride; however, Benjamin Bunny is quite at ease and collects some onions to take back to his aunt. He is nibbling lettuce when McGregor's cat wanders nearby, and the two little bunnies run and hide under a basket—the very basket on which the cat decides to nap. After five hours, Peter's uncle comes to look for them and must fight off the cat. After switching both bunnies for being disobedient, he walks them out the gate and returns Peter to his mother, who is so happy to have the onions and to see Peter recovered his clothing that she forgives him. (After all, Peter already had his punishment at the hands of his uncle.)

The Tale of Jemima Puddle Duck by Beatrix Potter. (1908). Frederick Warne & Co. 64 pages. Jemima Puddle Duck becomes quite annoyed when the farmer's wife removes her eggs and allows the hens to hatch them, so the duck decides to make a secret nest in the woods. There, she meets a polite fox who offers her his shed. The simple-minded duck is not at all suspicious that the shed is full of feathers, and she proceeds to lay nine large eggs. The fox watches over her nest when the duck returns to the barnyard each evening for food. One day, the duck agrees to bring some herbs and two onions to add to a sumptuous meal from the fox—never realizing that the fox intends to use the ingredients to make stuffed roast duck and a large omelet. When the farm dog, a collie named Kep, finds out what the silly duck is planning to do with the herbs and onions, he inquires on the whereabouts of the shed and trots off to enlist the help of two foxhounds. The three dogs chase the fox away, but the eggs are destroyed in the aftermath. However, the farmer's wife does allow Jemima Puddle Duck to hatch her own brood the next time.

Other best-selling picture books by Beatrix Potter include *The Tale of Squirrel Nutkin* and *The Tale of Tom Kitten*.

How the Grinch Stole Christmas by Dr. Seuss. (1957). Random House. 64 pages. Other Dr. Seuss books were included in the previous chapter under Easy-to-Read Books. However, this book is for more experienced readers, although younger children will certainly enjoy if you read it to them. The Grinch, whose heart is two sizes too small, lives with his timid dog, Max—alone in a cave on a cold mountain above the village of the cheerful Whos. The Grinch hates the holiday celebrations in merry Whoville, and he steals all the Whos' presents, decorations, and holiday food in order to prevent Christmas from coming. To his amazement, Christmas comes anyway, initiated by the joyous singing of the Whos. The Grinch discovers the true meaning of Christmas when the Whos include him in their observance of the holiday.

The Story of Babar, the Little Elephant by Jean de Brunhoff. (1937). Random House. 56 pages. *The Story of Babar* was first published in France in

1931 by the well-known author, artist, and storyteller Jean de Brunhoff. It was later translated into more than a dozen languages and was first published in the United States in 1937. In the first book, Babar loses his mother to a hunter, and he escapes into the big city where a rich old lady gives him money to buy a suit of clothes. She then takes him home to live in her elegant house. After two years, his cousins Arthur and Celeste run away to the city to find Babar, and he returns with them to the great forest, where the King of Elephants has recently died from eating a poisoned mushroom. Because Babar has become educated and wise from living among humans, the herd makes him the new king, and he selects Celeste to be his queen. At the end of the book, Babar and Celeste set off in a gorgeous yellow balloon on their honeymoon and further adventures.

Meet Babar and His Family by Laurent de Brunhoff. (1973). Harry N. Abrams. 32 pages. Although Jean de Brunhoff published a number of books about Babar, none ever attained bestseller status in the United States. However, his son, Laurent de Brunhoff, continued the series after his father's death, and one of his books is a bestseller. In *Meet Babar and His Family*, all the elephants live in Celesteville. Even the Old Lady has left the city to be close to her dear Babar, and she holds school for the children. The book highlights the seasonal activities of King Babar, Queen Celeste, and their children—Pom, Flora, and Alexander. In the spring, they prepare the garden; in the summer, they sail on the lake; in the fall, they go back to school; and in the winter, they have fun in the snow. All the other members of Babar's family and close friends make an appearance in this book: Cousin Arthur, Doctor Capoulosse, Zephir the monkey, and Cornelius— the oldest of the elephants.

Caps for Sale by Esphyr Slobodkina. (1940). HarperTrophy. 48 pages. One morning, a peddler walks around, trying to sell colorful caps from a tall, wobbly pile on his head. When he is unable to sell a single one, he walks out into the countryside and sits down under a shady tree. After carefully checking the caps, he falls asleep. When he wakes up, the caps are gone, and the tree is full of a band of mischievous monkeys—each wearing a cap. His efforts to outwit the monkeys and regain the caps are quite humorous.

Stellaluna by Janell Cannon. (1993). Harcourt. 46 pages. When an owl attack causes Stellaluna to lose grasp of her mother's breast, the baby fruit bat, not yet able to fly, falls into a soft nest with three baby birds. Mama bird cares for her (after evoking a promise not to hang upside down from the bottom of the nest), and Stellaluna learns to eat bugs and sleep at night (right side up). When all four of the little ones learn to fly, Stellaluna ventures too far from the nest and is once again lost. However, a flock of bats finds her asleep in a tree, and her mother emerges. After reuniting with Stellaluna, mother bat shows her how to use her night vision to find delicious mangoes.

The True Story of the Three Little Pigs by A. Wolf by Jon Scieszka, illustrated by Lane Smith. (1989). Viking Press. 32 pages. This parody of the familiar folktale "The Three Little Pigs" is sure to have children rolling with laughter. It is told from the wolf's point of view, who makes a case for being framed. He claims that, although he had a bad cold, he was baking a birthday cake for his dear old granny when he realized he was out of sugar. He went to his neighbor's straw house to borrow a cup when a sneezing fit made him huff and puff and blow the house down, killing the little pig inside. The wolf ate him because he could not leave a perfectly good ham dinner lying in the straw to spoil. He moved on to the next neighbor, a pig whose house was built of sticks, and a similar calamity allowed him to have a second helping. (He suggests that readers think of it as a big cheeseburger just lying there.) The third neighbor lived in a brick house, and when that pig insulted the wolf's granny, the wolf lost his temper and tried to beat the door down. The police arrived, and the reporters blew up the story for the newspaper, making him look big and bad— but he was framed! It was all because he had a bad cold, and he did not like to see food go to waste.

The Three Pigs by David Wiesner. (2001). Clarion. 40 pages. Another spoof of the popular folktale has a typical beginning. However, when the wolf blows down the first pig's house of straw, he blows the pig right out of the story frame onto the border of the illustration. One by one, the three pigs wander out of the confines of the story, and—after folding a page of their own book into a makeshift paper airplane—they go on an adventure to visit several other stories and take part in their plots. They even lure the cat and the fiddle out of their nursery rhyme to join them.

Walter the Farting Dog by William Kotzwinkle and Glenn Murray, illustrated by Audrey Colman. (2001). North Atlantic Books. 32 pages. Anyone who has owned a flatulent dog will break into raucous laughter with this book, which started as a joke between the two authors (one of whom owns the real Walter) and ended up at the top of *The New York Times* bestsellers list for more than a year. In the book, Betty and Billy find Walter—a fat gray dog with an apologetic look—at the pound (wonder why he was left there?) and bring him home. No matter what he eats, it gives him gas. Though the children love him regardless, the father decides Walter must go back to the pound the following day. Walter vows (to himself) to hold in his farts forever, but he soon begins to experience terrible stomach cramps. Burglars break in and mistake Walter's weakened condition for feebleness. They soon find out differently when Walter finally cuts lose with a hideous cloud of gas. The burglars drop their loot and stagger, choking and gasping, out of the house and into the path of a passing police car. When the family gets up the next morning, they see the bungled robbery and know that, somehow, Walter kept the family valuables safe, and so he gets to stay.

I love this book, and so do my adult students, but I do not think I could share it with a classroom of children for fear I would have a dozen or more Walter mimics for the rest of the school year. Some school libraries have even refused to purchase this book, so perhaps it is best shared by parents.

Walter the Farting Dog: Trouble at the Yard Sale by William Kotzwinkle and Glenn Murray, illustrated by Audrey Colman. (2004). Dutton. 32 pages. Walter, who seems to attract criminals, is equally funny in the sequel. His family is participating in a yard sale, but their table has no customers. Walter, who is farting contentedly near Father, wonders why. While Betty and Billy are elsewhere, a man offers $10 for Walter, and Father eagerly agrees. Walter is confused and sad, but when his new owner tells him he works as a clown at children's birthday parties, Walter figures he can help. The clown uses a fart catcher to capture Walter's gas, which he uses to inflate balloons—but not for a party. He is really a robber who takes the balloons into a bank and pops them to stun the guards and tellers. The clown (whose big red nose is really a gas mask) returns home with a sack of money, but when he decides to light a cigar before counting his loot, the place blows up. Walter scurries home, trailing $100 bills behind him. Of course, the police are not far away. After an attempted false arrest of Walter, they discover the real culprit when Walter leads them to his demolished hideout.

Diary of a Spider by Doreen Cronin, illustrated by Harry Bliss. (2005). Joanna Cotler. 40 pages. Through humorous diary entries, readers learn about typical events in the life of a young spider whose best friend is Fly. In one of his entries, Spider's mother tells him he is getting too big for his skin, so he molts and takes the old skin to school for show-and-tell. In another entry, he is concerned that he will have to eat leaves and rotten tomatoes when he has a sleepover with Worm. Because vacuum cleaners eat spiderwebs, readers also learn that Spider's school has vacuum drills (instead of fire drills). The adorable watercolor cartoons have funny asides in dialogue balloons that are the real punch lines of the entries.

Runny Babbit: A Billy Sook by Shel Silverstein. (2005). HarperCollins. 96 **pages.** Shel Silverstein worked for 20 years on this collection of silly poems, but the book was not published until six years after his death. All poems are written in a hilarious code using spoonerisms, or letter flipping. (The illustration of a bunny rabbit on the cover of *Runny Babbit* gives you the key.) Each poem stars Runny Babbit in a different persona. My favorite is Prince Runny who searches for Cinderella, trying to find a fit for the *slass glipper*, but he finds only *felly smeet* instead. In Runny's family are a *sother* and two *bristers* and of course a *dummy* and a *mad*. Other characters include Dungry Hog, Goctor Doose, Millie Woose, Ploppy Sig, Polly Dorkupine, Rirty Dat, Skertie Gunk, Snerry Jake, Toe Jurtle, and Pilly Belican (who owns the Sharber Bop), all of whom dwell in the green woods.

Watch that you do not get tongue-tied with uproarious words such as *bow snoots* (which are winter attire) and *sea poup* (which is something to eat, not flush). The comical line drawings provide visual clues, but poems still require some concentration to translate the silly phrases. Therefore, they are better enjoyed in *dall smoses*. The poems can provide many enjoyable hours of reading for school-age children, and preschool siblings can also gain key reading skills in phonemic awareness and segmentation with these spoonerisms that transpose the first consonants of adjacent words. (For more information on the importance and development of phonemic awareness, see Yopp, 1995, and the IRA position statement *Phonemic Awareness and the Teaching of Reading*, 1998).

Although they are more appropriate for older children, Silverstein has also published three additional collections of his clever and uproariously funny poems: *A Light in the Attic, Falling Up,* and *Where the Sidewalk Ends.*

Modern Fantasy

Modern fantasy is a term used to differentiate between the fantastical stories of very old traditional literature, which has no known authors, and the fantasy stories by known authors, which were first popularized by Hans Christian Andersen's tales (see Eitelgeorge & Anderson, 2004).

In addition to animal fantasy, three other categories of modern fantasy are represented in this chapter. In animated object fantasy, the main characters are inanimate objects such as toys, machines, or plants that have human characteristics. In enchanted journey fantasy, the main characters travel from the real world to fantasy realms. In supernatural fantasy, the main characters include beings that exist outside the natural world, such as spirits.

The Littlest Angel by Charles Tazewell, illustrated by Paul Micich. (1946). **Ideals. 28 pages.** In this supernatural fantasy book, the youngest angel in heaven is a 4-year-old boy from Jerusalem. He is quite homesick for earth, and he finds the transition from boy to cherub in the celestial kingdom a difficult one. He tries to fit in and do what is expected of him, but he seems to fail at every attempt. When he is called before the Understanding Angel, he pours out his heart and says he would not be so sad if only he could have his box of beloved possessions from home: a golden butterfly, a sky-blue egg, two white river stones, and the leather collar from his devoted dog. His wish is granted, but when it comes time for Jesus to be born on Earth, the Littlest Angel is once more sad because he has no gift for the Christ Child. Therefore, he adds his precious box to the pile of glorious gifts from the angelic hosts, but he is worried that God will think his gift too lowly. However, God is pleased because the Littlest Angel gave what he treasured most, and He transforms the box into the brilliantly shining star of Bethlehem.

The Giving Tree by Shel Silverstein. (1964). **Harper & Row. 56 pages.** In an animated object fantasy, an apple tree loves a little boy, and she provides a shady playground plus delicious apples for the rambunctious youngster. Making the boy happy is what makes the tree happy, but as he grows older, he no longer plays with her daily. When he is a teenager, he no longer wants to climb her trunk and swing on her branches. Instead, he needs money to make him happy, so she suggests he pick and sell her apples. He quickly takes her offer (but without a word of thanks) and leaves for a long time. The next time the tree sees the boy, he is a grown man, and he says he needs a house so he can have a family. She offers her branches for lumber to build a house, which he greedily cuts down and carts away (again without showing gratitude). When the boy is a middle-aged man (perhaps now retired), he returns, saying he wants a boat in which he can sail away because he is too old and sad to play with the tree. She suggests that he cut down her trunk to construct a boat. He quickly does so, but never looks back to see how sad the once beautiful tree—now reduced to a withering stump—looks. The boy returns one last time as a feeble old man and asks for a quiet place to sit and rest. The stump is aglow and happily offers herself because that is all she is now good for.

The message in this book is unclear: Does the story focus on the gift of giving and the serene acceptance of another's capacity to love? On the other hand, instead of a giving tree, does the story present the perils of having a friend who is a taker? Perhaps it is an allegory for humans taking Mother Nature and her bounty for granted. What is certain is that the book can generate much discussion on what are appropriate boundaries in friendships.

***The Missing Piece* by Shel Silverstein. (1976). HarperCollins. 112 pages.** In a highly imaginative fantasy, Shel Silverstein animates geometric objects such as circles and triangles with simple but appealing ink line drawings. The unhappy main character goes in quest of its missing piece that will make it a complete circle. As it rolls along the road, it finds missing pieces but discards one after another because none fits perfectly. As in Silverstein's other prose books, there is a story for children on one level and a message for adults on another. The symbolism points to people who spend their lives trying to find the right relationship to make them feel complete and fulfilled when they should be happy with themselves as they are.

***The Polar Express* by Chris Van Allsburg. (1985). Houghton Mifflin. 32 pages.** In an enchanted journey, a boy is awakened by the sound of a train in his front yard on Christmas Eve. He runs outside and catches the Polar Express, a train carrying children to the North Pole. After a trip with fabulous sights and delicious treats, the children arrive at the great city where elves make all the presents. They meet Santa, and he selects the boy (who narrates the story) to receive the first gift of Christmas. Instead of one of the beautifully wrapped presents, the boy asks only for a silver bell from Santa's reindeer. When it is midnight, Santa flies off in his heavily laden sleigh, and the children return home on the Polar Express; however, the boy has a sad trip home because the bell has fallen out of a hole in his pocket. In the morning, the boy finds the silver bell in a small box behind the Christmas tree, but only those who truly believe in Santa can hear its beautiful sound.

Zathura by Chris Van Allsburg. (2002). Houghton Mifflin. 32 pages. In an enchanted journey that catapults two brothers into a distant universe, Danny and Walter Budwing discover an old box of game boards in the park, and they take it home. After their parents leave for the evening, Danny becomes interested in an outer space–themed board with a path of colored squares leading to a purple planet called Zathura. A small green card pops out of the board's edge, and Danny reads that meteor showers require evasive action. When a giant meteor falls into their living room, the boys look through the hole in the ceiling and then out the windows and see only a dark sky with many stars. They are compelled to play the game to see if they can get back to Earth. Several dice-rolls later, they are scuttling to evade a homicidal robot and a scaly Zyborg pirate. Each play reveals a new threat, such as reversed polarity in one of the brother's gravity belts and a malfunctioning gyroscope. As ringed planets and spaceships swirl past the windows, they climb backward through the meteor hole in the ceiling, and with the help of a black hole that loops the brothers back to the park before they picked up the box, they are able to escape the dangerous journey to the planet Zathura. However, this means the game box is left in the park for some other unsuspecting child to pick up.

    Zathura is the third picture book by Chris Van Allsburg that has been made into a motion picture. The others are *The Polar Express* and *Jumanji*, which is the prequel to *Zathura.*

Cloudy With a Chance of Meatballs by Judi Barrett, illustrated by Ron Barrett. (1978). Atheneum. 32 pages. In a reverse enchanted journey in which the people in a fantasyland must travel to the real world, Grandpa tells his grandchildren about a faraway town called Chewandswallow. The residents did not have to buy and prepare food because the sky supplied all the food they wanted, three times a day. For example, it rained soup and juice, snowed mashed potatoes, and stormed hamburgers. One day the food started arriving more frequently and the portions became increasingly larger. When gigantic items of food stormed the town, the people glued together giant pieces of stale bread with peanut butter and sailed on those rafts to an ordinary land where people have to purchase and prepare their meals.

Mike Mulligan and His Steam Shovel by Virginia Lee Burton. (1939). Houghton Mifflin. 48 pages. In a nostalgic animated object fantasy, Mike Mulligan and his trusty red steam shovel, Mary Anne, accomplish many great feats. They help to dig great canals, mountain passes, long highways, large landing fields, and deep skyscraper basements. However, the introduction of gasoline, electric, and diesel shovels means that Mary Anne is old-fashioned, and nobody wants to hire them. Mike travels far out of the city to Popperville and promises that if they cannot dig the cellar for the new town hall in just one day, the town does not have to pay for their work.

The whole town gathers around the worksite to watch this determined pair in their race against time. Though Mike accomplishes his feat by sunset, he has forgotten to leave a way out for Mary Anne, so the people ask them to remain: Mary Anne is converted to the furnace for the new town hall, and Mike becomes the janitor.

The Jolly Postman by Allan Ahlberg, illustrated by Janet Ahlberg. (1986). **Little, Brown. 32 pages.** A jolly postman in fairy tale land delivers letters to the residents, who are all characters from a favorite fairy tale or Mother Goose rhyme. For example, the letter to Mr. and Mrs. Bear at Three Bears Cottage in The Woods is from Goldilocks, who apologizes for the trouble she caused. To make up for it, she invites Baby Bear to her birthday party. Alternate pages are actual envelopes with the letters tucked inside. The story of the postman's travels is told in verse with charming illustrations that are full of clever and hilarious details. Other examples of letters include one to Wicked Witch (of Hansel and Gretel), who receives a circular from Hobgoblin Supplies Ltd. that advertises products such as little boy pie mix. Jack (of beanstalk fame) also wrote to Giant during his vacation on a sunny island to thank him for the gold.

The Jolly Christmas Postman by Allan Ahlberg, illustrated by Janet Ahlberg. (1991). Little, Brown. 32 pages. The Ahlbergs created another masterpiece interaction book in *The Jolly Christmas Postman*. Inside the book's six envelopes are amusing letters and cards, including one addressed to Mr. H. Dumpty at Wincey Ward in Cock Robin Memorial Hospital, as well as to the Gingerbread Boy, Big Bad Wolf, and Little Red Riding Hood (with sound advice from Grandmother). However, this book also includes a few Christmas gifts, such as a jigsaw puzzle of Humpty Dumpty (to fit him together again), a tiny book, and an accordion-style peep show. As the Jolly Postman cycles through the fairy tale land delivering letters, the background shows Old King Cole's castle, a gigantic beanstalk, the dish and the spoon (running off to elope), and other favorite characters. Of course, the postman's last visit is to everyone's favorite character, Santa.

Realistic Fiction

The characteristics of realistic fiction are quite different from fantasy. The setting is a realistic location during either contemporary or historical times. The characters are realistic people—no talking animals or people with superhuman abilities. No magic or fantasy of any kind exists in this genre, and the plots typically reflect real-life situations, although the tone is often light and humorous.

Alexander and the Terrible, Horrible, No Good, Very Bad Day by Judith Viorst, illustrated by Ray Cruz. (1972). Atheneum. 32 pages. The youngest of three brothers gives a first-person account of his day, and everything goes wrong for him. It includes waking up with gum in his hair, having his best friend find another best friend, not finding dessert in his lunchbox, and accidentally calling Australia on his father's office phone. It is a terrible, horrible, no good, very bad day, which continues into the night. There are lima beans for supper and kissing on television, and Alexander is forced to sleep in his railroad-train pajamas—all of which he hates. He resolves several times to move to Australia, but he is later consoled by his mother, who tells him that other people have bad days, too (even in Australia).

Madeline by Ludwig Bemelmans. (1939). Viking Press. 48 pages. Petite Madeline and 11 other little girls live in an old house in Paris, France, that is covered with vines, where they are cared for and tutored by the loving Miss Clavel. Despite her size, Madeline fearlessly scoffs at the zoo's tiger, and she frightens Miss Clavel by balancing on top of the wall of a bridge over the Seine River. (This behavior gets her in serious trouble in the sequel, *Madeline's Rescue*.)

One night, Miss Clavel is awakened by plaintive cries, and Madeline is rushed to the hospital to have her appendix removed. Ten days later, Miss Clavel and her charges visit Madeline in the hospital. Not only does she have lovely flowers, candy, and new toys in her room, but she also has an interesting scar on her stomach. After the girls are all tucked in their beds that night, loud wailing in the dormitory again awakens Miss Clavel, but it is not a massive case of appendicitis—just envy.

Miss Rumphius by Barbara Cooney. (1982). Viking Press. 32 pages. When Alice Rumphius was a little girl, she had three goals: travel to faraway places, live by the sea, and do something to make the world more beautiful. As an adult, she travels the world, and when she grows older, she settles in a house by the seaside. She ponders a long while on what she might do to make the world more beautiful as she had promised her grandfather. Miss Rumphius loves flowers, especially blue-, purple-, and rose-colored lupines, and so she orders five bushels of lupine seed and walks about the countryside, sowing them. After all of the landscape near her home is blooming with lupines, she tells her young niece about her life. Little Alice in turn resolves to travel and retire by the sea, and she ponders how she might make the world more beautiful, continuing the cycle Miss Rumphius's grandfather began so many years ago.

Miss Nelson Is Missing! by Harry Allard, illustrated by James Marshall. (1977). Houghton Mifflin. 32 pages. The kids in Room 207 are the worst behaved class in the whole school. They ignore their soft-spoken teacher Miss Nelson, and they throw spitballs, fly paper airplanes, whisper, giggle, and make faces while she is trying to teach them (even during story hour). One day a vile substitute, Miss Viola Swamp, shows up instead of Miss Nelson, and the party is over. The Swamp scares the children into behaving, gives them loads of homework, and takes away story hour. The children search for Miss Nelson, but to no avail—even Detective McSmogg is baffled. When Miss Nelson returns a few days later, it is to a changed class. If you enjoy this book, you will also want to read *Miss Nelson Is Back*, and *Miss Nelson Has a Field Day*. Within the last few pages of each book, Allard reveals who the real Viola Swamp is.

Ira Sleeps Over by Bernard Waber. (1972). Houghton Mifflin. 48 pages. For any child who cannot sleep without a favorite blanket or toy, this book is sure to be a favorite. When Reggie invites Ira to spend the night, he is thrilled—until his big sister raises the question of whether he should take his teddy bear. As Ira gets ready for his first sleepover, he is torn between taking his teddy bear, Tah Tah, and leaving him home. He has never slept without him before, but his big sister says Reggie will laugh at him. His parents encourage him to take Tah Tah, but his sister continues to taunt him. After changing his mind several times, Ira finally decides not to take his teddy bear. However, when Reggie starts telling a scary ghost story after the lights are out, Ira has second thoughts. After Reggie scares himself with the story, he pulls his bear, Foo Foo, out of a drawer, and Ira slips next door to get Tah Tah.

Nonfiction

The preponderance of books that parents purchase are fiction; however, only about a quarter of a typical library's holdings for children are fiction. The rest of the children's books in libraries are nonfiction, of which informational books make up the bulk. An informational book is still considered literature, but in addition to providing entertainment, it also informs the reader by providing an explanation of factual material. It should come as no surprise that the all-time best-selling nonfiction picture books are about animals—and big scary ones at that.

Dinosaur Days **by Joyce Milton, illustrated by Richard Roe. (1985). Random House. 48 pages.** Children are enamored with animals, and they especially like extinct ones such as dinosaurs. In this well-structured book, the most common types of dinosaurs are introduced with descriptions and interesting facts. The name of each dinosaur is followed with the pronunciation and an explanation of what the scientific name means. For example, *Brontosaurus* means thunder lizard. They were thus named because they were so huge that when they walked, their enormous feet probably sounded like thunder. The colorful illustrations make it easy to imagine what these intriguing animals might have looked like. The book can also dispel any misconceptions that people coexisted with dinosaurs, which may arise from reading fantasy books with dinosaur characters.

Encyclopedia Prehistorica: Dinosaurs **by Robert Sabuda and Matthew Reinhart. (2005). Candlewick. 12 pages.** More than 35 stunning pop-up illustrations give readers an exciting view of what dinosaurs might have looked like during the Mesozoic period, and each illustration is accompanied with interesting facts and details on a particular species. Each of the six double-page spreads features a spectacular paper sculpture of a well-known dinosaur, including a gigantic Brachiosaurus, a spiked Anklyosaurus, and a detailed Tyrannosaurus Rex skeleton. Each double-page spread also contains as many as four foldout sections that open like miniature books and incorporate pop-ups as well as additional topics and facts on lesser known dinosaurs. Children will delight in seeing the colorful dinosaurs leap into three dimensions and in reading the most up-to-date information on more than 50 dinosaur species.

Hungry, Hungry Sharks by Joanna Cole, illustrated by Patricia Wynne. **(1986). Random House. 48 pages.** This introduction to sharks includes a great deal of information for a picture book. The beginning of the book provides some history of the species, explaining that they existed on earth before dinosaurs. The author provides interesting facts on all sizes of sharks, from the dwarf shark that is no bigger than a human hand to the whale shark, which is bigger than a bus and has about 3,000 teeth. Also included are facts on their food consumption; for example, a great white shark can eat a whole seal in a single bite, but the whale shark only eats tiny fishes. The author is careful to explain that few sharks eat people.

Inspirational

In addition to entertaining and informing young readers, books can also inspire them to feel good about themselves and to celebrate their successes as well as their uniqueness.

Today I Feel Silly and Other Moods That Make My Day by Jamie Lee Curtis, illustrated by Laura Cornell. **(1998). Joanna Cotler. 40 pages.** This comical look at children's common emotions can help to promote an understanding of moods. In zany verses, a frizzy-haired young girl acknowledges and describes different feelings by relating them to her everyday world. The author and illustrator are able to capture a number of feelings, such as angry, confused, cranky, encouraged, excited, frustrated, grumpy, hurt, joyful, quiet, sad, and, of course, silly. The girl talks about coping with the ups and downs of life (usually with a goofy striped cat by her side). A revolving insert at the back of the book allows children to identify their own feelings of the day, and it may help children to explore and identify their ever-changing moods.

I'm Gonna Like Me: Letting Off a Little Self-Esteem by Jamie Lee Curtis, illustrated by Laura Cornell. **(2002). Joanna Cotler. 32 pages.** With playful verse and jubilant illustrations (full of humorous details), a boy and girl alternate uttering declarations of pride at being exactly who they are, regardless of whether things are going right or wrong. When they try new things, work on their good behavior, play with baby brother, or help around the house, the clear message is that the key to feeling good is liking yourself because you are you.

You Are Special by Max Lucado, illustrated by Sergio Martinez. (1997). Crossway Books. 32 pages. The setting of this deeply touching story is Wemmicksville, a village created by the woodcarver Eli, whose workshop is on an overlooking hill. Eli has created all the wooden people in Wemmicksville to be unique; each has its own look and personality. In this tale about self-worth, Punchinello is a sad little man, whom Eli must help understand how special he is—no matter what other Wemmicks may think. Punchinello's opinion of himself grows increasingly more positive as he learns how to keep negative things the others say about him from sticking. (Wemmicks literally stick gold stars on those they think are winners and gray dots on those they think are losers.) The message for young readers is that regardless of how the world sees them, God made each of them special, and He loves them just as they are.

If Only I Had a Green Nose by Max Lucado, illustrated by Sergio Martinez. (2002). Crossway Books. 32 pages. In this sequel to *You Are Special*, Punchinello decides to have his nose painted green because it seems that everyone else is doing it, and he does not want to appear out of fashion. After he and his two friends have their noses painted, they enjoy looking down them at people who still have plain noses. Eventually, Punchinello learns that it can be difficult, foolish, and even dangerous to try to keep up with the latest fads, and that Eli, his maker, gave each Wemmick different characteristics on purpose. The message for young readers is that no matter how much they may want to fit in with the crowd, it is important to be who they were created to be.

The Trellis and the Seed by Jan Karon, illustrated by Robert Gantt Steele. (2003). Viking Press. 32 pages. When the Nice Lady plants a tiny seed, she says it will become a beautiful vine with sweet-smelling blossoms, but the seed does not believe her. The Nice Lady erects a tall trellis and waits for rain. After the rain, the seed sprouts, and the Nice Lady continues to talk of what it will become. However, the little sprout does not believe it will ever be anything but small, and the trellis looms far above. With more rain and a little time, the plant grows most of the way up the trellis. Then the Nice Lady applies some fertilizer, and the vine finally reaches the top. However, the vine gives up hope that it will ever produce flowers like the colorful foxgloves, hollyhocks, lavender, roses, and petunias that adorn the Nice Lady's garden. The Earth encourages the vine to wait, explaining that God's timing is different for the vine. Finally, the vine produces fragrant white flowers that bloom in the moonlight.

Yay, You! Moving Out, Moving Up, Moving On by Sandra Boynton.
(2001). Little Simon. 32 pages. This delightfully silly picture book features
unusual critters (for example, a cow doing yoga and a frog with an outboard
motor on his lily pad) that rejoice in the reader's recent success and offer some
possibilities that life has to offer. In a persistently upbeat tone, the rhyming text
alternates between cheering and questioning in the form of, "What will you do
next?" Questions are followed by options, such as adventure, travel, or enjoying
tranquil time at home eating chocolates. A text box on the first page has
"Congratulations" across the top and "To" and "From" below, making it clear this
book is intended for giving to someone to show pride and support in his or her
success, whether it be receiving a great report card, hitting a home run in Little
League, completing a first recital, or reaching an important birthday.

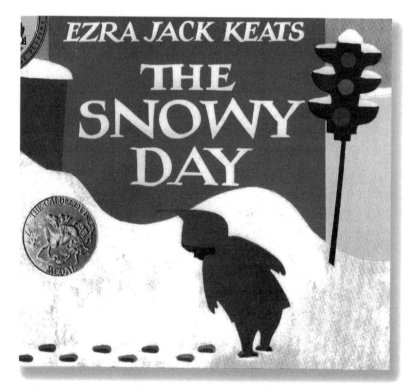

Book cover from *The Snowy Day* by Ezra Jack Keats. © 1962 by Ezra Jack Keats, renewed 1990. Used by permission of Penguin Group (http://www.penguin.com).

Chapter 7

Selecting Books to Supplement the Bestsellers

One of the recurrent themes in this book is that children love books about animals—in particular animal fantasy in which the characters act like humans. However, children have a strong attraction to animals in other genres as well, including realistic fiction, nonfiction, and poetry. Please do not think that because children love animals so much, you should only share animal books with them. After all, children love Snickers candy bars as well, but you would never allow them to eat only Snickers bars for breakfast.

Animal fantasy is delightful, but a steady diet of that genre alone will not prepare children for the reading demands they will face in school as they get older. Additionally, when children outgrow talking animals and they have not been exposed to the types of books older children prefer, then they may skip reading as a pastime in favor of television and video games, which would be their loss.

In chapter 1, I mentioned that if parents started when their children were born and read two of the bestsellers to them each month, by the time the children were 9 years old, they would have read all 200 books. However, I certainly hope that parents are going to read more than two books a month to their children. I recommend reading at least two or more new picture books each week and rereading a couple of their favorites each night.

In addition to the bestsellers, what kinds of books should you share with children? Just as you want children to eat a balanced meal each night, you should also want children to enjoy a balanced assortment of literature. I suggest starting with what is glaringly missing from the bestsellers lists—multicultural literature and nonfiction books—and, after that, finding magazines and Internet sites for diverse reading materials.

Multicultural Literature

While a number of best-selling books focus on the Christian religion, books focusing on other major world religions such as Judaism and Islam rarely make the bestsellers lists. In addition, nearly all of the bestsellers with human characters portray them as Caucasian, and yet the United States has very large populations of Latinos and African Americans as well as other ethnic groups. Children from diverse ethnic groups need to be able to identify with book characters that share their own religions and cultures, and children in the mainstream culture need to learn about the diverse people that live around them.

Books help readers understand people who may be different from them, thereby diminishing the possibility that they will prejudge those who appear different. Following are lists of picture books about various religions and cultures that are from a variety of genres, including traditional, realistic fiction, biography, and informational. Picture books in this chapter should be read in conjunction with books from the other chapters, not as isolated experiences, but rather as an integral part of your literature program. Just as children will encounter people from other cultures in their daily lives, books that focus on a variety of cultures should be part of their daily lives.

Islam

***Fasting and Dates: A Ramadan and Eid-ul-Fitr Story* by Jonny Zucker, illustrated by Jan Barger Cohen. (2004). Barron's Educational. 24 pages.** In this simple introduction to the Islamic festival of Ramadan and Eid-ul-Fitr, young children can follow a family as they fast each day, go to the mosque on the Night of Power, and enjoy a delicious feast.

***The Hundredth Name* by Shulamith Levey Oppenheim, illustrated by Michael Hays. (1997). Boyds Mills Press. 32 pages.** Salah, a boy living in Egypt, wants to lift his camel's sadness, so he prays that the camel will learn Allah's hundredth name, which is unknown to man.

***Magid Fasts for Ramadan* by Mary Matthews, illustrated by E.B. Lewis. (2000). Clarion Books. 48 pages.** Though Grandmother ages, she still has important lessons to teach about life as she asks her granddaughter to "Remember that."

Muslim Child: Understanding Islam Through Stories and Poems by Rukhsana Khan, illustrated by Patty Gallinger. (2002). Albert Whitman. 104 **pages.** This collection of stories and poems about Muslim children from a variety of backgrounds focuses on the celebration of holidays and practices of Islam.

Ramadan by Suhaib Hamid Ghazi, illustrated by Omar Rayyan. (1996). Holiday House. 32 pages. This book describes the celebration of the month of Ramadan by an Islamic family and presents the meaning and importance of this holiday in the Islamic religion.

Ramadan and Id al-Fitr by Diane M. Macmillan. (1994). Enslow. 48 pages. This book of holidays describes Ramadan and Id al-Fitr and provides a look into the Islamic culture of Mohammed, mosques, minarets, and the Koran.

Judaism

Elijah's Tears: Stories for the Jewish Holidays by Sydelle Pearl, illustrated by Rossitza Skortcheva Penny. (2004). Pelican. 63 pages. The prophet Elijah appears in five stories about Jewish holidays that include Hanukkah, Yom Kippur, Succot, Pesach, and Shabbat.

Golem by David Wisniewski. (1996). Clarion Books. 32 pages. A devout rabbi miraculously brings to life a clay giant who helps him watch over the Jews of 16th-century Prague.

The Little Room by Chaim Desnick, illustrated by Janet Zwebner. (2004). Pitspopany Press. 32 pages. When David the store owner realizes he has no free space for his Passover goods, he decides to use the little back room.

The Magic Dreidels: A Hanukkah Story by Eric A. Kimmel, illustrated by Katya Krenina. (1996). Holiday House. 32 pages. When an old lady swindles Jacob out of his magic dreidels, he tries to get them back in time for the family's Hanukkah celebration.

The Power of Light: Eight Stories for Hanukkah by Isaac Bashevis Singer, illustrated by Irene Lieblich. (1990). Farrar, Straus and Giroux. 87 pages. This collection of Hanukkah stories by a Nobel Prize winner provides rich descriptions of the miraculous power of light over evil.

Sammy Spider's First Hanukkah by Sylvia A. Rouss, illustrated by Janus Kahn. (1993). Kar-Ben. **32 pages.** After watching the Shapiro family celebrate the different nights of Hanukkah, Sammy Spider finds that in the end he gets to share the holiday with them.

Hinduism

Chachaji's Cup by Uma Krishnaswami, illustrated by Soumya Sitaraman. (2003). Children's Book Press. **32 pages.** Through stories told over a beloved old teacup, a boy learns about his family history and the Partition of India from his great uncle.

How Ganesh Got His Elephant Head by Harish Johari and Vatsala Sperling, illustrated by Pieter Weltevrede. (2003). Bear Cub Books. **32 pages.** This magical story tells how Ganesh, the son of Shiva and Parvati, was brought back to life with the head of an elephant.

Little Krishna by Harish Johari, illustrated by Pieter Weltevrede. (2002). Bear Cub Books. **48 pages.** This book relates adventures of the young Krishna, the Hindu god who was known as a child for his mischievous nature.

Buddhism

The Hermit and the Well by Nhat Hahn, illustrated by Vo-Dinh Mai. (2005). Plum Blossom Books. **36 pages.** In this autobiographical story, the author speaks of his childhood interest and commitment to Buddhism, which prompted him to visit temples and other places of worship, including a class field trip to a hermit living in the mountains.

I Once Was a Monkey: Stories Buddha Told by Jeanne M. Lee. (1999). Farrar, Straus and Giroux. **40 pages.** Six *Jatakas*, or birth stories, illustrate some of the central tenets of Buddha's teachings, such as compassion, honesty, and thinking clearly before acting.

Zen Shorts by Jon J. Muth. (2005). Scholastic. **40 pages.** Three children meet Stillwater, a giant panda who moves into the neighborhood and tells amazing tales about the value of material goods, the boundaries of good and bad, and what happens when one holds on to frustration.

African American

Bigmama's by Donald Crews. (1998). HarperTrophy. 32 pages. When Donald and his siblings visit Bigmama's house in the country, they find their relatives full of news, but the old place and its surroundings are just the same as the year before.

A Chair for My Mother by Vera B. Williams. (1984). HarperTrophy. 32 pages. After a fire destroys their home and possessions, Rosa and her mother and grandmother save coins until they can afford to buy one big, comfortable chair that all three of them can enjoy.

Coming on Home Soon by Jacqueline Woodson, illustrated by E.B. White. (2004). Putnam. 32 pages. During World War II, Ada Ruth's mother goes to Chicago, Illinois, where women are needed to fill the men's jobs, and the young girl and her grandmother wait every day for the letter that says that Mama will be coming home soon.

Flossie and the Fox by Patricia McKissack, illustrated by Rachel Isadora. (1986). Dial Books for Young Readers. 32 pages. A wily fox, notorious for stealing eggs, meets his match when he encounters a bold little girl in the woods who insists upon proof that he is a fox before she will be frightened.

John Henry by Julius Lester, illustrated by Jerry Pinkney. (1999). Puffin. 40 pages. John Henry, who is stronger than 10 men, races against a steam drill to cut through a mountain.

Tar Beach by Faith Ringgold. (1996). Dragonfly Books. 32 pages. In 1939, 8-year-old Cassie Louise Lightfoot flies above her apartment-building rooftop, which she calls the tar beach, and looks down on Harlem.

Asian American

Baseball Saved Us by Ken Mochizuki, illustrated by Dom Lee. (1995). Lee & Low. 32 pages. A Japanese American boy learns to play baseball when he and his family are forced to live in an internment camp during World War II, and his ability to play helps him after the war is over.

Grandfather's Journey by Allen Say. (1993). Houghton Mifflin. 32 pages. A Japanese American man recounts his grandfather's journey to the United States, which the author later retraces, and shares his grandfather's feelings of being torn by a love for two very different countries.

The Lotus Seed **by Sherry Garland, illustrated by Tatsuro Kiuchi. (1997). Voyager Books. 32 pages.** When she is forced to leave Vietnam, a young girl brings a lotus seed with her to the United States in remembrance of her homeland.

Moonbeams, Dumplings, & Dragon Boats: A Treasury of Chinese Holiday Tales, Activities, & Recipes **by Nina Simonds and Leslie Swartz, illustrated by Meilo So. (2002). Gulliver Books. 80 pages.** This book contains recipes, hands-on family activities, and traditional tales to inspire families to re-create the magic of Chinese holidays in their own homes.

My Name Is Yoon **by Helen Recorvits, illustrated by Gabi Swiatkowska. (2003). Farrar, Straus and Giroux. 32 pages.** Disliking her name as written in English, Korean-born Yoon (meaning shining wisdom) refers to herself as *Cat*, *Bird*, and *Cupcake* as a way to feel more comfortable in her new school and new country.

The Name Jar **by Yangsook Choi. (2001). Dragonfly Books. 40 pages.** After Unhei moves from Korea to the United States, her classmates help her decide what her new name should be.

Latino

Calling the Doves **by Juan Felipe Herrera, illustrated by Elly Simmons. (2001). Children's Book Press. 32 pages.** The author recalls his childhood in the mountains and valleys of California with his farm worker parents, who inspired him with poetry and songs.

Chato's Kitchen **by Gary Soto, illustrated by Susan Guevera. (1997). Paperstar. 32 pages.** To entice the *ratoncitos* (little mice) who have moved into the barrio to come to his house, Chato the cat prepares all kinds of good food: fajitas, frijoles, salsa, enchiladas, and more.

Family Pictures **by Carmen Lomas Garza. (2005). Children's Book Press. 30 pages.** The author describes, in both English and Spanish text and colorful illustrations, her experiences growing up in a Hispanic community in Texas.

Going Home by Eve Bunting, illustrated by David Diaz. (1998). HarperTrophy. **32 pages.** A Mexican family comes to the United States to work as farm laborers so their children will have more opportunities, but the parents still consider Mexico their home.

Hairs by Sandra Cisneros. (1997). Dragonfly Books. **32 pages.** These vignettes from the author's *The House on Mango Street* reveal intimate portraits of familial love and the diversity among us.

Too Many Tamales by Gary Soto. (1996). Putnam. **32 pages.** Maria tries on her mother's wedding ring while helping make tamales for a Christmas family get-together, but panic sets in when, hours later, she realizes the ring is missing.

Native American

Baby Rattlesnake by Te Ata, illustrated by Mira Reisberg. (1993). Children's Book Press. **32 pages.** Willful Baby Rattlesnake throws tantrums to get his rattle before he is grown, but he misuses it and learns a lesson.

Giving Thanks: A Native American Good Morning Message by Jake Swamp, illustrated by Erwin Printup, Jr. (1997). Lee & Low. **24 pages.** This description of a traditional Iroquois ceremony, the Thanksgiving Address, demonstrates the symbols of giving thanks to natural and spiritual elements in life.

How Rabbit Tricked Otter and Other Cherokee Trickster Stories by Gayle Ross, illustrated by Murv Jacob. (2003). Parabola Books. **78 pages.** This collection of 15 Cherokee tales introduces the trickster hero Rabbit, who is both charming and mischievous as he tricks others and is even tricked himself.

Jingle Dancer by Cynthia Leitich Smith, illustrated Cornelius Van Wright. (2000). HarperCollins. **32 pages.** Jenna, a contemporary Muscogee (Creek) girl in Oklahoma, wants to honor a family tradition by jingle dancing at the next powwow, but she does not have enough jingle bells for her dress.

Little Woman Warrior Who Came Back: A Story of the Navajo Long Walk by Evangeline Parsons Yazzie, illustrated by Irving Toddy. (2005). Salina Bookshelf. **32 pages.** Dzáníbaa and her family are captured by U.S. soldiers and taken to Fort Sumner in the New Mexico territory, where they are forced to walk to Bosque Redondo, a place where they encounter incredible hardship for four long years.

Thirteen Moons on Turtle's Back: A Native American Year of Moons
by Joseph Bruchac and Jonathan London, illustrated by Thomas Locker.
(1997). Putnam. 32 pages. This collection celebrates the seasons of the year
through poems based on the legends of Native American tribes such as the
Cherokee, Cree, and Sioux.

Nonfiction Books

Few books of nonfiction (which includes both informational books and
biographies) make the children's bestsellers lists, and yet they are among the
most interesting sources from which children can learn about their world—
certainly more entertaining than textbooks. Children do not typically self-select
nonfiction books for recreational reading, but when those books are shared
with children, they often include them among their favorites. Following is a list
of nonfiction books that young children will likely enjoy.

Biography

A Boy Called Slow by Joseph Bruchac, illustrated by Rocco Baviera. (1998).
Putnam. 32 pages. Sitting Bull, who eventually became a great Lakota Sioux
chief, was first named Slow, and this account tells of his efforts to outgrow his
childhood name and take his place as an adult among his people.

Charlie Parker Played Be Bop by Christopher Raschka. (1992).
Scholastic. 32 pages. This picture book biography introduces the famous
saxophonist and his special style of jazz, known as bebop.

Chocolate by Hershey: A Story About Milton S. Hershey by Betty
Burford, illustrated by Loren Chantland. (1994). Carolrhoda Books. 64
pages. In 1876, Hershey started his own candy business as a teenager, and he
eventually built a chocolate factory and a town in what was once a cornfield,
naming both after himself.

Harvesting Hope: The Story of Cesar Chavez by Kathleen Krull,
illustrated by Yuyi Morales. (2003). Harcourt. 48 pages. This book chronicles
the life of Cesar Chavez from age 10, when he and his family lived happily on
their Arizona ranch, to age 38, when he led a peaceful protest against California
migrant workers' miserable conditions.

Henri Matisse: Drawing With Scissors by Jane O'Connor, illustrated by Jessie Hartland. (2002). Grosset & Dunlap. 32 pages. This brief biography describes Matisse's changes in style, use of bright colors, and skill in various mediums during the Fauve movement in which he shifted from painting to cut-paper collage.

Reaching for the Moon by Buzz Aldrin, illustrated by Wendell Minor. (2005). HarperCollins. 40 pages. This Apollo 11 astronaut, who was the second human to walk on the moon, recounts episodes in his life that influenced his choice to become part of the space program.

Snowflake Bentley by Jacqueline Briggs Martin, illustrated by Mary Azarian. (1998). Houghton Mifflin. 32 pages. Wilson Bentley was a self-taught scientist who photographed thousands of individual snowflakes in order to study their unique formations.

Teammates by Peter Golenbock, illustrated by Paul Bacon. (1992). Voyager Books. 32 pages. This book describes the racial prejudice experienced by Jackie Robinson when he joined the Brooklyn Dodgers and became the first black player in Major League baseball; the acceptance and support from his white teammate, Pee Wee Reese, is highlighted.

Health

I Miss You: A First Look at Death by Pat Thomas, illustrated by Lesley Harker. (2001). Barron's Education. 32 pages. This book helps children understand that death is a natural part of life, and that grief and a sense of loss are normal feelings following a loved one's death.

My Bodyworks: Songs About Your Bones, Muscles, Heart and More! by Jane Schoenberg and Steven Schoenberg, illustrated by Cynthia Fisher. (2005). Crocodile Books. 32 pages. Young children will discover how their bodies work when they read and sing along with fun and fact-filled songs.

Open Wide: Tooth School Inside by Laurie Keller. (2000). Henry Holt. 40 pages. Dr. Flossman is excited to meet his incoming class of 32 pupils—eight incisors, four canines, eight premolars, and 12 molars (including the four wisdom teeth)—who learn about things such as brushing, flossing, dentin, pulp, and tooth decay.

"Where Did I Come From?" by Peter Mayle, illustrated by Arthur Robins. (2000). Lyle Stuart. 48 pages. This easy-to-understand book for young children describes the reproductive process from intercourse to birth.

Animals

Antarctic Ice by Jim Mastro, illustrated by Norbert Wu. (2003). Henry Holt. 32 pages. Photographs and text describe the varied animal life on the coldest continent, focusing on the Adâelie penguin, Weddell seal, and Orca whale.

Bats by Gail Gibbons. (2000). Holiday House. 30 pages. This book describes different kinds of bats, including their physical characteristics, habits, and behaviors, as well as human's efforts to protect them.

From Caterpillar to Butterfly by Deborah Heligman, illustrated by Bari Weissman. (1996). HarperTrophy. 32 pages. A caterpillar comes to school in a jar, and the class watches as it grows and changes into a chrysalis and then a beautiful butterfly that flies out of the jar.

The Giraffe by Christine Denis-Huot, illustrated by Michel Denis-Huot. (1993). Charlesbridge. 27 pages. This colorful book provides interesting facts about the tallest living animal in the world, such as how many bones are in a giraffe's neck and how they sleep.

A Mother's Journey by Sandra Markle, illustrated by Alan Marks. (2005). Charlesbridge. 32 pages. This book chronicles the female Emperor penguin from the time she lays her first egg through her epic journey to open sea as she seeks food and finally returns with a full belly and regurgitates for her newly hatched chick.

What Do You Do With a Tail Like This? by Robin Page, illustrated by Steve Jenkins. (2003). Houghton Mifflin. 32 pages. This book explores the many amazing things animals can do with their ears, eyes, mouths, noses, feet, and tails.

Young Naturalist's Handbook: Insect-lo-pedia by Matthew Reinhart. (2003). Hyperion. 48 pages. This book highlights 26 families of insects and provides a general description of insect characteristics, bodies, and behavior.

Science and Math

From Seed to Pumpkin by Wendy Pfeffer, illustrated by James Graham Hale. (2004). HarperTrophy. **40 pages.** This simple book explains the stages in the development of a seed into a pumpkin, and it includes easy recipes and interesting experiments.

The Greedy Triangle by Marilyn Burns, illustrated by Gordon Silveria. (1995). Scholastic. **40 pages.** In this introduction to polygons, a dissatisfied triangle convinces a shape shifter to make him a quadrilateral and later a pentagon, but he discovers that where angles and sides are concerned, more is not always better.

How Do Apples Grow? by Betsy Maestro, illustrated by Giulio Maestro. (1993). HarperTrophy. **32 pages.** This book describes the life cycle of an apple from its initial appearance as a spring bud to a tree with fully ripe fruit.

The Moon Book by Gail Gibbons. (1998). Holiday House. **28 pages.** This book describes how humans have observed and explored the moon over the years and includes information on its movement, phases, and eclipses.

Stars! Stars! Stars! by Bob Barner. (2002). Clarion Books. **32 pages.** This lively book takes readers on an imaginary ride through outer space to visit distant planets and dazzling stars.

What Is the World Made Of? All About Solids, Liquids, and Gases by Kathleen Weidner Zoehfeld, illustrated by Paul Meisel. (1998). HarperTrophy. **32 pages.** In simple text, the author presents the three states of matter—solid, liquid, and gas—and describes their attributes.

What's Out There? A Book About Space by Lynn Wilson, illustrated by Paige Billin Frye. (1993). Grosset & Dunlap. **32 pages.** With interesting text and colorful illustrations, this book provides basic information about the sun, moon, and planets that make up our solar system.

History and Geography

The Man Who Walked Between the Towers by Mordicai Gerstein. (2003). Roaring Brook. **32 pages.** In 1974, French aerialist Philippe Petit strung a tightrope between the two towers of the World Trade Center, and he spent an hour walking, dancing, and performing high-wire tricks a quarter mile in the sky.

My Freedom Trip by Frances Park and Ginger Park, illustrated by Debra Reid. (1998). Boyds Mills Press. 32 pages. The authors tell the exciting but bittersweet account of the escape of their mother from North Korea to freedom when she was a child.

We the Kids: Preamble to the Constitution of the United States by David Catrow. (2005). Puffin. 32 pages. This humorously illustrated book looks at the Preamble, providing an accessible introduction to the United States' founding ideals.

When Washington Crossed the Delaware by Lynne Cheney, illustrated by Peter Fiore. (2004). Simon & Schuster. 40 pages. On Christmas night in 1776, General George Washington led the main body of his army across the Delaware River and launched a surprise attack on the British, a pivotal battle of the U.S. Revolutionary War.

Where Do I Live? by Neil Chesanow, illustrated by Ann Iosa. (2005). Barron's Educational. 48 pages. This book explains to children exactly where they live, starting with their room, their home, their neighborhood, their town, their state, their country, the planet earth, the solar system, and the Milky Way galaxy.

Magazines for Young Children

In addition to books, children enjoy colorfully illustrated magazines and other periodicals. Following are a few of the best magazines published for children. The primary topics, targeted age groups, subscription address, and website follow each title. By visiting the websites, you can learn more about their topics, view sample pages, and subscribe.

Chickadee: Science and nature; ages 4–8; 25 Boxwood Lane, Buffalo, NY 14227, USA; https://secure.indas.on.ca/bayard

Highlights for Children: General interest; ages 2–12; PO Box 269, Columbus, OH 43216, USA; http://www.highlights.com

Humpty Dumpty's Magazine: General interest and health; ages 4–6; Children's Better Health, PO Box 567, Indianapolis, IN 46206, USA; http://www.cbhi.org/magazines/humptydumpty

Jack and Jill: General interest and health; ages 7–10; PO Box 10003, Des Moines, IA 50340, USA; http://www.cbhi.org/magazines/jackandjill

Kids Discover: Variety of themes; ages 6–12; 170 Fifth Avenue, 6th Floor, New York, NY 10010, USA; http://www.kidsdiscover.com/teachFR.htm

Ladybug: General interest; ages 2–6; PO Box 50284, Boulder, CO 80323, USA; http://www.cricketmag.com/ProductDetail.asp?pid=5&type=

Nick Magazine: Humor; ages 6–14; PO Box 0945, Des Moines, IA 50340, USA; http://shop.nickjr.com/product/index

Ranger Rick: Nature and environment; ages 6–12; National Wildlife Federation, 8925 Leesburg Pike, Vienna, VA 22184, USA; http://www.nwf.org/kidspubs/rangerrick

Internet Sites

The Internet contains valuable information about children's literature, and some websites even contain the full text of stories that are free for downloading, for example, the websites Project Gutenberg (which archives electronic text of works in the public domain), Aesop's Fables, and Hans Christian Andersen's Stories. You can use the Internet for many things: additional sources of reading material, information on favorite authors and illustrators, ideas for literature response activities, lists of suggested books to read, reviews of new books, and information on award-winning books. Some recommended websites follow.

Aesop's Fables (with full text)
http://AesopFables.com
Authors and Illustrators
http://www.fairrosa.info/cl.authors.html
Beginning With Books
http://www.clpgh.org/clp/bwb/bestbaby.html
Book Activities
http://www.sdcoe.k12.ca.us/score/cyk3.html

Book Awards

http://www.ala.org/ala/alsc/awardsscholarships/literaryawds/literaryrelated.htm

Children's Choices Award

http://www.reading.org/resources/tools/choices_childrens.html

Children's Songs (with lyrics and melodies)

http://www.kiddidles.com/mouseum

Content Information

http://www.MarcoPoloSearch.org

Hans Christian Andersen's Stories (with full text)

http://www.andersen.sdu.dk/vaerk/hersholt/index_e.html

How to Raise a Reader

http://www.ala.org/alsc/born.html

Multicultural Book Selection

http://teacher.scholastic.com/products/instructor/ multicultural.htm

Jim Trelease on Reading Aloud

http://www.trelease-on-reading.com

Multicultural Books

http://www.cynthialeitichsmith.com/summerreading.htm

Preschoolers' Book Activities

http://www.preschoolrainbow.org

Project Gutenberg (with full text)

http://www.gutenberg.net

Rhymezone

http://www.rhymezone.com

Teachers' Choices Awards

http://www.reading.org/resources/tools/choices_teachers.html

Traditional Tales (with full text)

http://www.rickwalton.com/folktale/folktale.htm

Glossary

ABC book Another term for alphabet book

alphabet book A concept book that presents the letters of the alphabet (also called *ABC book*)

animal fantasy A type of fantasy story in which main characters are *anthropomorphic animals* who talk, experience emotions, and have the ability to reason as humans

animated object fantasy Stories with characters that are inanimate objects—such as toys, plants, or machines—that have life-like characteristics

anthropomorphic animals Animal characters that can talk, experience emotions, and have the ability to reason as humans

Big Book A book that is enlarged to about four times its normal size, used by a teacher with a group of children

biography A nonfiction work describing the life, or part of the life, of a real individual

board book A book for very young children, consisting of sturdy cardboard pages that have a glossy wipe-off finish

collage An art form in which shapes are cut or torn from materials, such as paper and fabric, and are assembled and glued on a surface

concept book A picture book that presents numerous examples of a particular concept such as the alphabet, numbers, colors, shapes, and opposite words

concept of word Recognition that a written word is a string of letters bounded by spaces

concepts of print The directionality of written language; for example, a page is read from top to bottom, lines are read from left to right, and books are read from front to back

diphthong vowels Two vowel sounds in the same syllable

double–page spread Two facing pages in a book; typically refers to an illustration that spreads over two adjacent pages

easy–to–read book A book written specifically on the level of a beginning reader

enchanted journey fantasy A fantasy story that begins in the real world, but the main character is soon transported to another world, which is often an enchanted realm

genre Categories of books (and other media), such as fantasy and realistic fiction

grocery store books Books about cartoon, comic book, TV, and movie characters that are typically sold in grocery stores and large chain stores

informational book A trade book with the primary purpose of informing the reader by providing an in-depth explanation of factual material

interaction books Books that contain lift-up flaps, textured pages, moving parts, scented pages, or pop-ups; also called *participation books*

invented spelling Spelling words the way they sound when the standard spelling is not known; for example *kat* for *cat*

juvenile novel A novel written specifically for children; also called junior novels

language experience account (LEA) A child's dictated account of something he or she has experienced, recorded by an adult and used for reading instruction

lap reading An experience in which a child sits in an adult's lap, and they look at a book together

letter–name correspondence Knowledge of the various forms of a letter (upper- and lowercase, print and manuscript) and the name by which it is called

letter–sound correspondence Knowledge of which letter (or letter cluster) represents specific language sounds

library binding A sturdier binding than regular hardcover trade books

listening prediction activity A comprehension activity in which children listen to a story and make predictions about what might happen next (used with unfamiliar stories with a strong plot)

lowercase letters Letterforms that are not capitals (also called small letters)

merchandise books Books that are published to promote sales of theme park or movie tickets and the merchandise associated with them such as dolls and toys

modern fantasy A fiction story with highly fanciful or supernatural elements that would be impossible in real life; has a known author (as compared with *traditional fantasy*, which has no known author)

multicultural literature Cross-cultural literature that includes books by and about peoples of all cultures

nonfiction Books that are not fiction, such as biography and informational

participation book Another name for an *interaction book*

pattern book A book containing repetitive words, phrases, questions, or some other structure that makes it predictable

phoneme The smallest unit of speech that distinguishes one word sound from another, such as the *c* in *cat*

phonemic awareness Awareness of the sounds (phonemes) that make up spoken language

phonological awareness Awareness of the constituent sounds of words, which include phonemes, syllables, and rhymes

picture book A book that conveys its message through a series of pictures with only a small amount of text

picture storybook A picture book that contains a plot with the text and illustrations equally conveying the story line

poetry Verse in which word images are selected and expressed to create strong, often beautiful impressions, typically using rhyming words

public domain Status of works not protected by copyright laws, usually because of age

reading The process of obtaining meaning from print in an interaction between the reader and written language, in which the reader reconstructs a message from the writer

realistic fiction A type of fiction story that does not have any element of fantasy or magic

sense of story structure Knowledge that stories have a beginning in which the author introduces the characters, setting, problem, and goal; a middle that consists of several attempts to overcome the problem (or several events that lead to the solution); and an ending in which the problem is resolved

series Three or more books that have some unifying element, such as characters or theme, typically written by the same author and produced by the same publisher

speech-to-print match The ability to match spoken words to their written counterparts

supernatural fantasy Stories with main characters that include beings that exist outside the natural world, such as spirits

trade book Any literature book that is marketed to libraries, wholesale booksellers, retail bookstores, and book clubs

traditional literature Stories, songs, and rhymes with unknown authorship that were passed down orally from one generation to the next before being written down; also known as *folk literature*

uppercase letters The capital letters, also called big letters

visual literacy The ability to interpret illustrations and other graphic stimuli

voice-pointing procedure An activity whereby the reader points under each word as it is spoken; used to determine speech-to-print match

wordless picture book A book in which the story is revealed through a sequence of illustrations with no—or a very few—words

References

Anderson, N.A. (2006a). *Elementary children's literature: The basics for teachers and parents* (2nd ed.). Boston: Allyn & Bacon.

Anderson, N.A. (2006b). *The 200 all-time bestselling picture books.* Paper presented at the annual meeting of the International Reading Association, Chicago.

Anderson, N.A., & Eitelgeorge, J.S. (in press). *Animal fantasy: The neglected genre.*

Anderson, R.C., Hiebert, E.H., Scott, J.A., & Wilkinson, I.A.G. (1985). *Becoming a nation of readers: The report of the Commission on Reading.* Washington, DC: National Institute of Education.

Botzakis, S., & Malloy, J.A. (2006). International reports on literacy research: Emergent readers. *Reading Research Quarterly, 41,* 394–403.

Brinson, S.A. (1997). Literature of a dream: Portrayal of African American characters before and after the Civil Rights movement. *The Dragon Lode, 15,* 7–10.

Clay, M.M. (1979). *Stones: The concepts about print test.* Exeter, NH: Heinemann.

Connor, C.M., & Tiedemann, P.J. (Eds.). (2005). *International Reading Association–National Institute for Child Health and Human Development Conference on early childhood literacy research: A summary of presentations and discussions.* Newark, DE: International Reading Association.

DeCasper, A.J., Lecanuet, J.P., Busnel, M.C., & Granier-Deferre, C. (1994). Fetal reactions to recurrent maternal speech. *Infant Behavior & Development, 14,* 159–164.

Eitelgeorge, J.S., & Anderson, N.A. (2004). The work of Hans Christian Andersen—More than just fairy tales. *Bookbird: A Journal of International Children's Literature, 42*(3), 37–44.

Grover, E.O. (1971). Foreword. *Mother Goose.* Northbrook, IL: Hubbard Press.

Harris, T.L., & Hodges, R.E. (1995). *The literacy dictionary: The vocabulary of reading and writing.* Newark, DE: International Reading Association.

International Reading Association. (1998). *Phonemic awareness and the teaching of reading* (Position statement). Newark, DE: Author.

International Reading Association. (2002/2003). A rabbit's tale: Peter Rabbit celebrates his 100th birthday. *Reading Today, 20*(3), 42.

International Reading Association. (2005). *Literacy development in the preschool years* (Position statement). Newark, DE: Author.

Karoly, L.A., Greenwood, P.W., Sanders, M., & Chiesa, J. (1998). *Investing in our children: What we know and don't know about the costs and benefits of early childhood interventions.* Santa Monica, CA: RAND.

Kirkpatrick, D.D. (2000, October 26). Literary sleuth casts doubt on the authorship of an iconic Christmas poem. *The New York Times.* Retrieved April 2, 2007, from http://www.nytimes.com/2000/10/26/arts/26NIGH.html

Lawson, D.V. (1972). *Children's reasons and motivation for the selection of favorite books.* Unpublished doctoral dissertation, University of Arkansas.

Mohr, K.A.J. (2002, November). *Children's choices: A comparison of book preferences between Hispanic and non-Hispanic first-grade students.* Paper presented at the meeting of the College Reading Association, Philadelphia, PA.

Mohr, K.A.J. (2006). Children's choices for recreational reading: A three-part investigation of selection preferences, rationales, and processes. *Journal of Literacy Research, 38,* 81–104.

Morrow, L.M. (2005). *Preschool curriculum throughout the years.* Paper presented at the meeting of the International Reading Association and National Institute for Child Health and Human Development on early childhood literacy research. Newark, DE: International Reading Association.

Peterson, G.C. (1971). *A study of library books selected by second-grade boys and girls in the Iowa City, Iowa Schools.* Unpublished doctoral dissertation, University of Iowa.

Richards, J.C., & Anderson, N.A. (2003). What do I see? What do I think? What do I wonder? (STW): A visual literacy strategy to help emergent readers focus attention on storybook illustrations. *The Reading Teacher, 65,* 442–444.

Roback, D.E. (2003, March 24). The bestselling children's books of 2002. *Publishers Weekly.* Retrieved December 1, 2003, from http://publishersweekly.reviewsnews.com

Roback, D.E., Britton, J., & Hochman, D. (2001). All-time bestselling children's books. *Publishers Weekly, 248*(51), 24–32.

Roskos, K.A. (2005). *How storybook instruction impacts early reading development.* Paper presented at the meeting of the International Reading Association and National Institute for Child Health and Human Development on early childhood literacy research. Newark, DE: International Reading Association.

Strickland, D.S., & Shanahan, T. (2004). Laying the groundwork for literacy. *Educational Leadership, 6,* 12.

Truitt, E. (1998, September 3). The book industry's best-seller lists: What are they, and why do they matter so much? *Slate.* Retrieved September 30, 2006, from http://slate.msn.com/?id=3504

Vukelich, C., & Christie, J. (2004). *Building a foundation for preschool literacy: Effective instruction for children's reading and writing development.* Newark, DE: International Reading Association.

Yopp, H.K. (1995). A test of assessing phonemic awareness in young children. *The Reading Teacher, 49,* 20–30.

Name and Title Index

Subject Index

A

ABC BOOKS, 40–41, 66; definition of, 129

AFRICAN AMERICANS, 72–73, 119

AGE LEVELS, xv, 11; 1–2, 31–51; 3–4, 53–73; 5–6, 75–95; 7–8, 97–113; infants, 31–51

ALPHABET BOOKS, 40–41, 66; definition of, 129

ALPHABET SOUP, 35

ALPHABETIC KNOWLEDGE, 13, 40

ANIMAL BOOKS, 33–36; nonfiction, 124; popularity of, 5; realistic, 35–36, 58, 68

ANIMAL FANTASY, 53–62, 82–90, 97–103; definition of, 129

ANIMATED OBJECT FANTASY, 62–64, 104; definition of, 129

ANTHOLOGIES, 8–9

ANTHROPOMORPHIC ANIMALS, 5; definition of, 129

ASIAN AMERICANS, 119–120

B

BEARS, 36, 42, 61, 64, 70, 80, 84–85, 87

BEDTIME STORIES, 31–33

BEST-SELLING PICTURE BOOKS: for children ages 3–4, 53–73; for children ages 5–6, 75–95; for children ages 7–8, 97–113; for infants and children ages 1–2, 31–51; supplements to, 115–128; trends in, 4–5

BIG BOOKS, 2; definition of, 129

BIOGRAPHY, 122–123; definition of, 129

BOARD BOOKS, 7, 31; definition of, 129

BOOK CLUBS, 6

BOOKS: finding, xv, 10–11

BUDDHISM, 118

BUGS. *See* insects

BUNNIES. *See* rabbits

C

CALDECOTT MEDAL, 73

CARNIVAL BOOK CLUB, 6

CATS, 35, 61

CHICKENS, 34, 50, 89

CHRISTIAN BOOKS, 46–48, 65, 112

CHRISTMAS STORIES, 57, 61, 70, 78, 90, 93, 99, 105–106

COLLAGE, 42; definition of, 129

COLORS, 41–42

CONCEPT BOOKS, 40–46, 66–68, 94–95; definition of, 129

CONCEPT OF WORD, 14, 22; definition of, 129

CONCEPTS OF PRINT, 2, 14, 18–19; definition of, 129; inventory of, 20–21

COUNTING BOOKS. *See* numbers

D

DEVOTIONAL BOOKS, 46–48

DINOSAURS, 39, 61, 81, 110

DIPHTHONG VOWELS, 66; definition of, 129

DIRECTIONALITY, 18

DOGS, 49, 54, 60, 78, 81, 88, 101–102

DOUBLE-PAGE SPREAD, 33; definition of, 130

DUCKS, 49, 58, 68, 86–87, 89, 99

E

EASTER STORIES, 58, 88

EASY-TO-READ BOOKS, 7–8, 76–82; characteristics of, 76; definition of, 130

MOTHERS, 37, 78, 80, 87, 100, 119, 124

MULTICULTURAL LITERATURE, 116–122;
definition of, 131

N

NATIVE AMERICANS, 121–122

NO CHILD LEFT BEHIND (NCLB) ACT,
xiv–xv

NONFICTION, 97, 110–111; definition of,
131; supplemental, 122–126

NUMBERS, 42–43

NURSERY RHYMES, 70–71

O

OPPOSITES, 38–39

ORAL LANGUAGE DEVELOPMENT, 13, 38

P

PAPERBACK BOOKS, 6

PARTICIPATION BOOKS, 48–51; definition of,
131

PATTERN BOOKS, 29, 55; definition of, 131

PHONEME, 15; definition of, 131

PHONEMIC AWARENESS, 13, 40; definition of,
131

PHONOLOGICAL AWARENESS, 13, 40;
definition of, 131

PICTURE BOOKS, 1–11; definition of, 131;
formats of, 5–10. *See also* best-selling
picture books

PICTURE STORYBOOKS, 97; definition of, 131

PIGS, 39, 43, 45, 56, 101

POETRY, 90–91; definition of, 131

PREDICTIONS: activity on, 25–26; questions
on, 3

PRINT KNOWLEDGE, 13

PROJECT GUTENBERG, 70

PUBLIC DOMAIN, 69, 127; definition of, 131

PUPPIES. *See* dogs

Q–R

QUESTIONS: for reading aloud, 2–3, 18, 26,
28

RABBITS, 36–37, 45, 48–49, 58–59, 98–99, 103

READING: definition of, 13, 131; teaching,
with literature, 13–29; terminology in, 18

READING ALOUD: benefits of, 1–3; involving
children in, 3–4; routine for, 28–29

READING FIRST INITIATIVE, xiv–xv

READING VOCABULARY, 38

REALISTIC FICTION, 72–73, 97, 108–110;
definition of, 131

RELIGION: Buddhism, 118; Christianity, 46–48;
Hinduism, 118; Islam, 116–117; Judaism,
117–118; Native Americans, 121–122

RETELLING: strategy for, 27

RHYMING TEXT, 2

S

SCHOLASTIC BOOK CLUB, 6

SCIENCE, 125

SERIES: definition of, 132

SHAPES, 43–44

SONGS, 71–72

SPEAKING VOCABULARY, 38

SPEECH-TO-PRINT MATCH, 14, 22; definition
of, 132; inventory of, 23–24

STORY RETELLING STRATEGY, 27

STORY STRUCTURE, SENSE OF, 14, 25;
definition of, 132

SUPERNATURAL FANTASY, 104; definition of,
132

T

TEXT SELECTION: supplemental, 115–128;
tips for, xvi

THIRTY-MINUTE NIGHTLY ROUTINE, 28–29

TRADE BOOK, xiii; definition of, 132

TRADITIONAL LITERATURE, 69–71; definition
of, 132

TRAINS, 62–63, 82

TRENDS: in best-selling books, understanding, 4–5
TROLL BOOK CLUB, 6
TRUMPET BOOK CLUB, 6

U

UPPERCASE LETTERS, 14; definition of, 132
UTAH EDUCATION NETWORK, 35

V

VISUAL GAMES, 91–94
VISUAL LITERACY, 56, 92; definition of, 132

VOCABULARY: in easy-to-read books, 8; types of, 38
VOICE-POINTING PROCEDURE, 2; definition of, 132

W–Z

WEBSITES, 127–128; Alphabet Soup, 35; eBay, 11; Project Gutenberg, 70; Utah Education Network, 35
WHALES, 37, 68, 83, 124
WORDLESS PICTURE BOOK, 5; definition of, 132
WORDS: first, 38–40
ZOO STORIES, 35, 80–81